UTOPIA AND OTHER PLACES

UTOPIA

AND

OTHER PLACES

RICHARD EYRE

BLOOMSBURY

First published in Great Britain 1993
Bloomsbury Publishing Ltd, 2 Soho Square, London W1V 5DE

Copyright © 1993 by Richard Eyre
The moral right of the author has been asserted

A CIP catalogue record for this book is available
from the British Library

ISBN 0 7475 1380 5

Typeset by Hewer Text Composition Services, Edinburgh
Printed in Great Britain by Clay Ltd, St Ives plc

TO SUZE AND LU

CONTENTS

Preface   ix

PERSONAL   1
Long Shadows   3
Acting Properly   72

PEOPLE   107
Granville-Barker   109
Olivier   117
Peter Brook   121
Ken Campbell   124
Ian Charleson   130
Ion Caramitru   134
Tony Harrison   142

PLAYS   149
Guys and Dolls   151
Richard III   157

POLITICS   165
My Country Right or Wrong   169
What's the National Theatre For?   173
What Are the Arts For?   178
Bonfires on the Moon: Theatre of the Nineties   182

Epilogue   203
Acknowledgements   205

PREFACE

When I was younger I wrote bad poetry, a play that was put on at Hampstead Theatre Club and shown by Granada TV, a film that was never made, a successful version of *A Christmas Carol*, and an unsuccessful version of *High Society*, but for many years I wrote nothing at all.

In becoming Director of the National Theatre I found myself a sort of muted celebrity – at least in the sense of being invited (and refusing) to go on *Wogan*, asked for my opinion on whales and rain-forests, courted by charities, and begged to contribute pieces to newspapers. It's an irony that after years of idleness, at least on the writing front, I should have started writing when I had little enough time left from my day (and night) job. However, I am an insomniac and much of many of these pieces was written during hours that might more profitably have been spent sleeping, and if there is a consistent colour to the writing, perhaps it is drawn from the cold light of dawn.

Georges Simenon said that he never sat down to write without feeling physically sick. I can understand how he felt. I have never been able to write except at someone else's suggestion, and even then I have to be goaded into it, but few of the important things in my life have happened on my own initiative. If I admire writers above all creative people, perhaps it's self-interest – I can't do my work until they've done theirs. Of course I admire the talent of the writers I like, but I admire as much the courage of those who earn a living from it – the solitary ordeal of facing a blank sheet of paper that stares implacably back at you requires the fortitude of the true professional.

As a writer, I'm a dilettante. I'm normally impatient of dilettantes; I don't like to hear actors talking of 'turning their hand to a bit of directing', and I've always refused offers of directing operas for the same reason. I have seen the faces of writers when I have told them I am doing a book, a mixture of scepticism and weariness. Not another one, they think.

I had never imagined that I would write a book, certainly not *The National Theatre – My Struggle*. I was approached by Liz Calder, who I can now call my publisher, but up to then called a friend. She said she'd read a piece that I had written and had I thought of writing a book? About what, I said. Oh I don't know, she said, about how you got into the theatre, perhaps. And that's how I came to write about my parents, who had little, if anything, to do with the theatre either before or after I got into it.

My mother's illness had prevented me for many years from communicating with her, and, when Liz approached me, my father had just died. I felt an overwhelming sense of unfinished business; there was a lot I wanted to say to them, and there was a lot I wished they could say back. I didn't want to write about them with the triumphant irony of the survivor; on the contrary, writing about them seemed a way of trying to get in touch with them. At first I felt curiously constrained, but when my mother died earlier this year I found that I could speak to them as I had never done in their lifetimes. It's sad that it happened posthumously, but in writing about them I learned a little more about them, and a lot more about myself. You write to discover what you think.

The word 'I' occurs too frequently in these pieces to pretend that they're not autobiographical, even when they purport to take a disinterested stance. This is, therefore, a sort of autobiography and, as such, an imposition; it is a demand to spend several hours in the company of a person who will attempt, however diffidently, to grab your collar and talk remorselessly, in a voice marked by the accent of self-doubt, about himself. The pieces in this book are by no means a revelation of my private life, or an itemised record of my professional life in the theatre and in television, but they do reflect a growing interest in the form of the medium in which I mostly work; becoming Director of the National Theatre has concentrated my mind wonderfully in that direction.

Robert Frost said that poetry is what gets lost in translation. I have become increasingly interested in the 'untranslatable' element in the theatre, the part that isn't a surrogate for television, that isn't prose to be read standing up, the part that can't be translated from stage to screen; the part that is, in a word, theatrical. This word is generally used in a pejorative sense to imply something camp, frivolous and superficial. For me it's come to describe a kind of theatre that exploits the unique properties of the medium – its use of space, of light, of speech, of story-telling: its *theatreness*. This can take many forms; it can be experienced in the spectacle of an anguished vicar standing on an illuminated, cross-shaped stage in *Racing Demon*, or a king struggling for reason and dignity while strapped in a strait-jacket, as much as in the image of an angel ascending over the head of a man dying of AIDS or in the surrealistic poetry of Robert Lepage's production of *A Midsummer Night's Dream*.

In my work I've always depended on the kindness of patrons – Clive Perry at Leicester and Edinburgh, Stuart Burge at Nottingham, Margaret Matheson at the BBC, and Peter Hall at the National Theatre. Without their generous encouragement my life would have taken a much less interesting course. As a writer I have had suitors rather than patrons: as well as Liz Calder, there have been David Hare, without whom I wouldn't have written about acting, the *Listener*, the *London Review of Books*, the *Guardian*, the *Independent*, the *Independent on Sunday*, the *Sunday Telegraph*, Neil Astley of Bloodaxe Books, Peggy Butcher of Methuen, Nick Hern of Nick Hern Books, and Lyn Haill of the National Theatre. Some of the pieces that they commissioned appear in this book.

I hope their courtship has been justified.

I've called this book *Utopia and Other Places*. 'Utopia' means, in Greek, 'not a place', that is – 'nowhere'. It's an imaginary island, and it serves as a powerful metaphor in life and art and politics. However sceptical we are of it in public, all of us privately believe in a utopia, in a form of perfectability, however temporary; it may be in love, in marriage, at work, in society, or in religion. Even when the available evidence is so strongly against its existence, we continue to seek this elusive territory.

Oscar Wilde is celebrated for having said, 'A map of the world which does not include utopia is not worth even glancing at.' I don't believe that we can avoid carrying this map within us, but I've nevertheless always been cautious about using it – in religion and politics, it's been such a costly and wasteful expedition in terms of human life. In the theatre, however, the search for utopia is a familiar, even necessary, part of the process: to rehearse a play in the company of good actors, sharing a sense of common purpose, mutual respect, and pleasure in each other's company, is to come as close as you can to finding the elusive spot on the map marked 'utopia'. I've never quite found it, but I've had a lot of fun looking.

PERSONAL

LONG SHADOWS

'Everything the Power of the World does is done in a circle.'

– American Indian saying

I

Our parents cast long shadows over our lives. When we grow up we imagine that we can walk into the sun, free of them. We don't realise until it's too late that we have no choice in the matter; they're always ahead of us, forever old.

We carry them within us all our lives, in the shape of our face, the way we walk, the sound of our voice, our skin, our hair, our hands, our heart. We try all our lives to separate ourselves from them and only when they are dead do we find we are indivisible.

We grow to expect that our parents, like the weather, will always be with us. Then they go, leaving a mark like a handprint on glass or a wet kiss on a rainy day, and with their death we are no longer children.

When my parents' death came I was in my late forties, and I was unprepared, even with the years of rehearsal, for adulthood. 'You're the one in the red jacket now,' said a friend of mine. 'You're in the Thin Red Line.' And another said, 'Now you're an orphan.' I hadn't known what to expect. Novelists and anthropologists talk of 'rites of passage', but we lack the casual ceremonies, the rituals, and the social habits that give death and grief the familiarity of shared experience and the comfort that we are enduring a 'rite of passage'. Perhaps that's what adulthood means: dealing with desolation alone. Grief and romantic love share some of the same

3

metaphors – heartache and heartbreak, for instance. They seem fanciful from a distance but turn out to be precisely observed descriptions of physiological phenomena. When we're young we rehearse these feelings by falling in and out of love and with odd, teasing glimpses of our parents' mortality.

I had just sat down on a plane, and was beginning to buckle my safety belt, when my name was called out and I was asked to leave the plane. I walked down the aisle, off the aircraft, along a corridor to an office, where I was confronted by an official whose face was moulded into a formal expression of compassion. 'Your mother has had an accident.' I had known this from the instant my name was called. I loved her at that moment with a ferocious intensity, which persisted when I saw her in the hospital, and when she recovered we never quite slipped back into our mutual wariness. My love for her had been dormant, waiting to be goaded into expression by illness or death. The threat of loss made me feel my affections were being tested like an electric current, measured and quantified by both of us.

In the years after, although I didn't see a lot of my mother, I never forgot the vivid, searing moment of pain when I thought I had lost her. It defined with exactness, and guilt, the shape of the feelings that should have existed before. It persisted like the feeling in a phantom limb, shadowing me whenever I saw her subsequently.

I once visited a leper colony in Kuala Lumpur. It was a Sunday morning and patients in varying degrees of decay, from all over the encampment, were going to church. There was a hut set aside for Gurkha patients, ex-soldiers, who paraded, eight of them, in a line outside their hut. Leprosy eats away the body, eventually causing joints and limbs to wither, atrophy and vanish. The soldiers were in tropical uniform – knife-edge creases on their shorts and shirts, sharp caps perkily set on the side of their heads. They stood at ease. Their sergeant brought them to attention, they saluted, and, as eleven o'clock struck, a bugler played the Last Post. Their drill was faultless. Only three of the eight men had two legs, none of them had the full complement of fingers, and all of them lacked part of an arm. Those without a hand raised their upper arm and elbow in a salute, the phantom hand perfectly placed one inch above the right eyebrow. The gesture was no less real for being imagined.

I had little hint of my father's mortality until shortly before his death. When I was eight I saw him on his knees, late at night after a party, talking to the dogs, groaning that he was about to die. I wasn't fooled – even at that age I knew the difference between death and drink, and he was always as indestructible as he was inaccessible. When he did become ill and vulnerable, he wanted to get to know me, and I wanted to get to know him, and we both knew that we had left it too late.

The loss of my parents gets dimmer day by day, and the pain, or the displaced love, translates into curiosity. I find that, far from wanting to distance them from me, I want to draw them closer. I want to know more about them: I am trying to learn what is an accident of nature and what is their indelible legacy. I want to know who I am.

When we lose our memories, we are less than ourselves; in that sense, we are what we remember. What we don't remember we try to reclaim through photographs and anecdotes, the verbal and visual chronicles of a family. We collect photographs as evidence, as if we were preparing for a day when we would examine, explain and judge our past. The day never comes, but we still preserve the photographs, as if their existence provided us with a sort of immortality.

A teacher in a school in Brazil gave his illiterate pupils photographs of themselves and they started to learn to read. Perhaps the photographs of ourselves can be used as a teaching aid – to reveal ourselves to ourselves. I have a photograph of myself in a pram, chubby, round, happy face, torrents of blond curls. I'm none the wiser. I seem to have discarded that person, and his successors, through the years. Childhood, school, university, work: shuffled off like the skin we lose almost as it grows upon us.

Memory is the key to our inheritance. It's said we remember everything; our problem is retrieving it. We talk about the 'dim recesses' of our memory as if the mind were a house that we could wander through at will. Our childhood occupies part of that house – a dense succession of rooms shot through with shafts of milky golden sunlight connected by long bleak corridors pitted with pools of dead water. We can shine a light on to these dark pools but we'll see only dead insects; unhappy childhood memories drift to the surface unasked and unsought for. We want to see childhood as a paradise, free from fear, but childhood's not a paradise, lost or otherwise. It's like one long Sunday afternoon – boredom punctuated by apprehension.

I was born during the War. To talk of 'the War' nowadays is to define oneself as a child of the forties as surely as printing one's birth certificate, but at least until recently you could be confident of sharing a common language; the Falklands and the Gulf have forced us not to take so much for granted. It was 'the War' that provided the basic grammar for my parents' lives.

There are three acts to my family's drama: 'Before the War', 'After the War' and a prolonged and still unresolved coda called 'Growing Up and Growing Apart'. 'Before the War' was for my mother a gilded era of intense social activity and friendships: holidays in France, Italy, Switzerland, New York; riding, golf, skiing, dancing and parties. She had an air of easy laughter that can be seen in countless photographs ('enjoying a joke') – but her laughter looks natural and unforced. She was described by a social correspondent as the 'soul of merriment', and I don't believe it was a flattering exaggeration. For my father: social privation, parental tyranny and naval discipline from the age of thirteen.

'During the War': vivid, intense, passionate, a difficult act to follow. It is one of the consequences of war that life will never be the same for those who are involved and that the casualties are not always the participants. When my parents were together they lived as if it might have been their last time together, and when they were apart my father faced the possibility of U-boat attack in the Baltic, and my mother the certainty of the casual cruelty of her father-in-law with whom she was obliged to live. And she gave birth to two children – my sister and then me.

Our parents' lives are always seen in the past tense; their children's in the future. The period of the War was invoked with mathematical regularity through our childhood and their memories wound up and regulated our emotional clock. It was unquestionably the time of their lives.

I remember little of the War. A gas mask: a perforated snout with huge round eyes and a flat flappy nose; a 'Donald Duck' mask issued to small children. I remember even the smell and the feel of the rubber, flabby like an inner tube. I realise now that I would have been too young to have worn it, too young even to have been issued with one. So it must have been long after the War and this is a kind of guileless alchemy, turning fiction into fact. I'm not sure I'm a reliable witness to my past.

My first memory. I am standing by our gate, a solid, high, wooden gate which clanged with a hollow thud, never quite shut, every time echoing in a flag-stoned yard by a large cherry tree, which in my memory is always, of course, in flower, handfuls of rich pink blossoms. Perhaps in the beginning it wasn't there. Perhaps it was planted by my mother.

I am playing, perhaps I'm pushing a furry golden horse on wheels. It has a long, soft, bushy tail and it belongs to my sister. I am two years old. The gate opens and there stands the darkest man I've ever seen: skin like bark, thick black stubble, large black eyes. When he speaks I can't understand him, and I run to my mother. She speaks to him, words that I don't understand. She gives him something. Money, perhaps. He goes. I am crying.

The man I remember was an Italian ex-prisoner of war who was looking for work, odd jobs, labouring or gardening. It was years before I could explain his presence, years before I knew that he had been freed from a prisoner-of-war camp a few miles from our village, and it's not until now, trying to parse this infant memory, that I can acknowledge that the thing I really remember is my mother's fear. And her Italian. She spoke Italian to him and I never heard her speak a word of the language again.

There was no compulsion on my mother to conceal her knowledge of a foreign language, but it might as well have been so. Living in a small village in Dorset, Italian was an encumbrance, which dropped away with the passing years; not wanted on voyage.

The Russian poet Joseph Brodsky tells the story of his mother, during Stalin's purges, concealing her knowledge of French for fear of betraying her class origins: 'One day I found her with a French edition of my works. We looked at each other; then she silently put the book back on the shelf . . .' In our country the offence of being the wrong class is never mortal, but it's not possible to grow up in England without learning that you have to negotiate the codes of class with the ingenuity of a spy on foreign territory. You learn the role: when to conceal your origins, when to display them. It's as essential a part of an English child's social anatomy as learning that you can get some food by saying 'please', and more by saying 'thank you'. Most of us are damaged by this process and even though the wounds can be cauterised they are never superficial.

I used to play in the gutted fuselage of a large military glider with the children who lived down the lane. My friends were known to my parents as the 'village' boys. They found me out pretty quickly. I said 'lunch' when I should have said 'dinner', 'dinner' when I should have said 'tea', and 'tea' when I should have kept quiet. I tried to pass for one of them and was teased by my father for talking with their accent. He called them 'the electors'. They were different from us, he said. This confused me. Far from being my inferiors my friends seemed my superiors in every way: more agile, more confident, more knowledgeable. They knew about 'vartin'. 'No,' said my father, 'farting.' And he illustrated his point loudly. He could be a rough teacher, but I was a keen pupil and I quickly learned the skills of recognition and camouflage.

Life is all loose ends; fiction has shape and coherence, and unravels meanings through epigrammatic anecdotes. There is one incident in my childhood that has the force of a fictional parable. As a rare experiment in performing the role of the conventional parent, my father decided to teach me to play cricket. He bowled and he batted left-handed, but was otherwise exclusively right-handed. He had been taught by his left-handed father, who saw no reason to accommodate nature's error in giving him a right-handed son. When my father taught me to play cricket he passed on his inheritance, and I learnt left-handed too. At the time it seemed natural enough that he made me follow his shadow, even if nature itself was in rebellion against it. Only with the advantage of hindsight does it seem such an uncomfortably resonant cautionary tale. I've often wondered what I would have taught my son if I'd had one.

Like my father, I am exclusively right-handed, but thanks to him I am as unable to bowl with my right hand as I am to meet another English person without consciously attuning my ear to their accent and their vocabulary. The ex-Prime Minister recently revealed that 'class is a communist concept'. She'd obviously not been in West Dorset in the fifties, but maybe she'd have regarded what I saw as a sort of secular Calvinism, the world divided into those who had entered an earthly heaven, and those who would never gain admittance.

In the myth Cadmus sows the dragon's teeth and reaps a harvest of armed men, who fight among themselves and destroy each other. My father's harvest was a lifelong discord with his son. Beyond that his legacy is that I am quick to anger which vanishes like a summer shower, I am stubborn, and I am reluctant to make moral judgements – at least on private matters.

He was a small but strongly built man, with almost Nordic,

snow-blond hair (he was known as Snowy), but his face was indelibly English, all nose and chin. I have his chin but not his nose. He was vain, and with his longish, slightly feathered hair, his colourful ties, his double-breasted, pin-striped suits, he was dapper as a bird, a chaffinch, perhaps.

My mother was handsome, bright-eyed and bright-skinned, confident and assertive, but it was a confidence that was like a skin laid over the bones of a nature that was hesitant, shy and over-eager for approval. She was always generous, even if she often seemed uncertain how to express it. Neither parent had tranquillity in their make-up. Later in his life my father hated travelling, but it did not quell a restless, febrile character. As for my mother – she loved travelling but, as in so many other things, she deferred to him.

Most children dream at some time that they are adopted. I used to dream that I was a changeling, and sometimes I think that my father wished that I could have been. My mother played the peacemaker. She used to say, 'I just want everyone to be happy,' and, as if to teach by example, was always cheerful, in public at least. Like the shape of my face, I've inherited my professional optimism from her. In the rehearsal room I am almost invariably accompanied by constant good spirits. It doesn't always come easily to me, and I'm not sure that it did to my mother, but it's a role to be played, a necessary one for a director, who can never professionally be too far removed from Dr Johnson's dictum on second marriage: the triumph of hope over experience. I don't think it was too far removed from my mother's feelings about her first and only marriage.

II

My mother was born in 1921 in London, in what was then Chelsea
and is now called the Fulham Road. Her parents were in their
thirties when they married, and she was an only child. Her mother
had been an actress before she married, my only genetic link with
the theatre. She acted under a name that sounds as implausible now
as it probably did then, Malise Sheridan. According to my father,
whose testimony was sometimes blinded by wishful thinking, she
had eloped with a racing driver whose initials were H.S. For years
I imagined this to be the raffish figure of Henry Segrave who stood
in front of a gleaming Sunbeam in my *Wonder Book of Daring Deeds*,
having broken the world speed record. I now realise that he would
have been about four at the time that my grandmother married,
so I must reconcile myself to the truth, as always less alluring
than fiction. The truth is that she eloped with an amateur racing
driver whose initials were G.S. – Guy Sebright, and she decided
to become an actress, which presumably caused as much grief to
her parents as her elopement.

I don't think she was a particularly good actress. Her first, and
greatest, success was in a play called *Diplomacy*, a long-running,
West End 'society drama' adapted from Sardou's four-act play
Dora. It starred Gerald Du Maurier, Owen Nares, and my
grandmother's friend, Gladys Cooper. The run of this play is
well documented in her scrapbook. Du Maurier stares insolently

at the camera, a cigarette holder dangling from one languid hand, the other reaching out for a drink being offered by the maid, who is crouching in an awkward curtsey. The maid was my grandmother and I think the photo is a fair metaphor for her professional career.

The part of the maid in *Diplomacy* was, however, no conventional 'Will-that-be-all-sir?' maid. On the contrary, according to the *Sketch*:

> Miss Sheridan is playing one of the comparatively few servants' parts which give the player a real chance, and she is making the most of her opportunities. Her performance is all the more interesting in that it marks her first appearance on the professional stage. She has to use four tongues – English, French, German and Italian – and is equally at home in each.

The play ran in London for eighteen months and then transferred to Broadway, where the production had the same success.

She was always a flamboyant dresser. A friend of my mother's described her to me: on a walk to pick blackberries she was dressed in a purple cloak with a buttonhole of artificial violets. I don't think she picked many blackberries.

She had something of a personal success, or at least her costume did, in *Under Cover:*

> Whatever the merits or otherwise of *Under Cover* – personally I enjoyed it immensely – the frocks are 'bully'. Most striking of all is Miss Malise Sheridan's sleeveless evening gown of red-gold tissue with its whole-skin, sable shoulder straps and swathed, sheath-like bodice, the material forming is caught into a loop just below the right hip and then develops into the square, sable-edged train.

I can't help thinking that something has been lost from theatre criticism over the last seventy-five years, not to mention costume design.

Like millions who were not at the Somme or at Passchendaele or in the Dardanelles, her life was indelibly blighted by the Great War. Her three brothers were all killed in action, and her marriage failed to survive the War. My mother told me that my grandmother remembered nothing of her first husband – or at least she never spoke of him, but she had never forgotten her three brothers. She had few relatives and her death, shortly after my mother's marriage, made my mother's status as an only child seem more than usually desolate.

She continued to act, another maid in *The Girl from Upstairs*, 'She spared no effort to keep things briskly moving'; a small part in a minor Maugham, *Love in a Cottage*, but at the end of the War she relinquished her career and her stage name to marry a naval officer called Charles Royds. I have a beautiful photograph of him: it is mostly occupied by a huge ice cliff, which towers above a minutely small figure of a man standing alongside his sledge, his figure no higher than an inch on the photograph. It is like looking down the wrong end of the telescope, time and distance making him like an insect on another planet.

III

Before he married, my maternal grandfather was a Polar explorer on Scott's first Antarctic expedition, responsible for the work of the men on shore and the internal workings of the ship, *HMS Discovery*. A few years ago it used to be possible to see his ship, moored alongside the Embankment just down-river from Waterloo Bridge, when you looked out of the office of the Director of the National Theatre: a rangy, elegant, black, three-masted, one-funnelled, wooden steam yacht. I have a leather-bound calendar on my desk; the day, the date and the month can be changed by turning little milled wheels. There is an inscription on the back:

DISCOVERY

THIS WAS THE CHARTER OF HER LAND

RULE BRITANNIA

The ostensible purpose of the Discovery Expedition to the Antarctic was scientific: meteorological, zoological, ornithological, botanical, biological, geological, geographical. Their real purpose was declared in the traditional pantomime ceremony of 'Crossing the Line' held as they passed over the Equator:

NEPTUNE: Have I the honour of addressing the Captain?
CAPTAIN: You have.

NEPTUNE: And what may be the Captain's name?
CAPTAIN: Captain Robert F. Scott.
NEPTUNE: Where are you bound?
CAPTAIN: To the South Pole.
NEPTUNE: Oh aye.

Their purpose, whether for science or glory, was to reach the South Pole before any other explorers. They never did reach the Pole, and by the time of the second expedition in 1910 my grandfather was too weary, or too unambitious, or perhaps too disenchanted with Scott, to make the second, fatal, attempt. Even before they landed in the Antarctic they charted undiscovered territory, the *Discovery* making a discovery in good earnest:

> For the first time in its long life, the great ice barrier had been looked on by human eyes . . . thousands of penguins crowded to see us: poor beasts, I wonder what they think we are?

They did reach further towards the Pole than anyone had been before, pulling their own sledges by hand after the death of their dogs, and nearly dying themselves in the effort.

They were extraordinarily young. When they set out they were described by the *Daily Mail*, in a style that is all too recognisable, as 'The Babes in the Wood'. They were young, you see, and their ship was wooden . . . Scott, then a Lieutenant Commander, was thirty-three. They were mostly, like my grandfather, naval officers and ratings, but they included among the crew of forty-seven a few civilian scientists, including my grandfather's friend the doctor, zoologist, scientist and artist Edward Wilson, who died later on Scott's second expedition. As well as looking after the ship, my grandfather was responsible for meteorological observations, for assisting the botanist Koettlitz, and for playing the piano, the pianola, and the harmonium. He was twenty-five years old when they left Portsmouth in August 1901.

I have my grandfather's journals written, mostly meticulously, in conditions which sometimes beggar belief. The ship is rolling in a gale, the ink is spilled, the cabin is leaking; a blizzard howls outside the hut, the temperature outside freezes the breath, the fingers have frostbite; the writing becomes perhaps a little spidery but still strong, and still legible. The leather-bound books are now quite fragile; each time I open them they shed more shards of their bindings like dry cigars.

Like him, I write a journal. I can't be absolutely confident that I'll never publish any or all of it, but I try to write it as if there was no one looking over my shoulder. It is as hard to keep an honest record of one's feelings as it is to take one's own photograph, and it involves a similar contrivance: it's difficult to avoid the pose of forced naturalness. It is not a matter of 'being yourself', but of being as truthful to the self-deceiving you as well as the artlessly innocent you. As John Updike says in his autobiography, 'What I have written strains to be true but nevertheless is not true *enough*.'

In my grandfather's journals you are always conscious of his intended audience, his family, and now I'm no less a part of that audience than his brothers and the clusters of cousins that he refers to as the 'girls'. I remember one of them from my childhood, his sister Jess. She was less tall than he was, but still monumental at six foot or so, and red-haired as he was and my own sister is. She remained unmarried and by the time I knew her was formidably eccentric. When she came to stay the house would shake as if possessed by a large poltergeist; countless times during the night, she noisily rearranged the furniture in her room, huge chests-of-drawers and tallboys, all subject to her mysterious whims. She was never in the wrong, and took this stance to such an extreme that I once discovered her burying the remnants of a china cup and saucer in the garden to avoid admitting that she had broken it.

Her brother wrote his journal as a testament; he knew that he might not return from his journey. He doesn't present himself as a man without fear, or without a sense of the danger that he was facing. If he has a purpose, a consistent vein, it is to demonstrate that the explorers were far from being extraordinary creatures coping with extreme circumstances. The wonder, if there was wonder, was in their ordinariness. Only once in the two years that he records does intemperance break through the self-control. In June, during the long winter of 1902, he is reading *Through the First Antarctic Night* by an earlier explorer, Dr Cook (even if he did winter in the Antarctic and reached the North Pole, Cook was known as 'a liar and a gentleman', an American Munchausen) and is 'thoroughly disgusted with it'. He spits indignantly at the descriptions of brooding over loneliness, weeping over sweethearts, and growing hair long out of sheer laziness. Seething with disapproval, he quotes great swatches of Cook's elegiac, mournful, and sometimes despairing account. I am bound to say that Cook's account does not strike me as exaggerated, in fact much of it seems remarkably vivid and all too plausible. But then I have never had to confront, and never could, what he describes as 'the everlasting white silence', to which my grandfather adds an almost audibly derisive shriek of exclamation marks – '!!!!!'. 'What we shall continue to do,' he writes, 'is to behave like ordinary human beings . . . The winter cannot be all joy and comfort, and no one could expect it, but with the help of a little tact, a little self-denial, and a cheery face, most of the monotony and discomfort can be overcome.' Is this courage? Is this stoicism? Or is it wilful lack of imagination?

The tone of the start ('At Sea') is characteristic, but its jauntiness didn't last much below the Equator:

The correct way to start this journal, which is for the benefit of my family, relations and friends, would be, at least some would imagine, 'Well, girls!!' but that would hardly do, so I say, gentlemen and ladies, the following pages are going to be written for you to read and see how we fared and what we did since leaving you, it was only yesterday and it seems years . . . Partings are always more or less painful, and I am thankful to think that the work and continuous bustle has kept one from thinking.

There was, mostly, enough work, and enough bustle. Blizzard winds, temperatures of minus 60°F, back-breaking sledge-loads dragged across ice floes, glaciers, crevasses and vast white desert wastelands of snow. The pain, the loneliness, the tiredness, and above all the cold, are reported with an uninflected simplicity which is all the more powerful for being understated and unself-pitying.

FRIDAY. −33°. Taking observations was absolute agony, as the wind cut through all our clothes. Time after time I thought my nose was gone and although it never went quite, it was all but and hurt like blazes, and feels as raw as beefsteak now.

MONDAY. Have taken to wearing my nose guard. I can't afford to be careless of that prominent feature on my face.
   The daylight is coming on a pace (sic), and at noon observations can be taken without a lamp. It was −57° at noon, and it had been as low as −62° or 95° of frost. What I call pretty chilly!!! One can't help laughing when one thinks of a sore throat and cold in England and thinking how one doesn't dare show one's nose out of doors.

The journey down was comparatively uneventful, if you are undisturbed by dealing with gales in a sailing ship and constant leaks due to poor construction: 'May the man who threw this ship together have bad dreams.' For my grandfather there was the constant routine of standing his watch, monitoring changes in the weather and in the crew (fortnightly measurements of the officers' weights, the dimensions of their chests, waists, biceps, forearms) and trawling daily for plankton to be examined by himself and Koettlitz under the microscope. A crustacean was named after him: *Roydsis formosa*.

There was little leisure time, but what there was was filled by writing letters, playing cricket on the deck, debates, or perhaps mere arguments, about insanity and suicide ('no result as usual'), the rights of women ('I have no opinion'), whether flying fish have wings, and the relative merits of seal, penguin and sea leopard. When they entered Antarctic waters the hunting instinct was allowed full play, the male ego hungry for expression, and an orgy of killing left the ship like a 'regular butcher's shop'.

The piano and the pianola ('The Flying Dutchman' a constant favourite: 'A ripping piece with plenty of go') were played most days and somewhere after the Equator the first sing-song was held in the Ward Room, with melancholy results: 'Talent is wanting in the singing line . . .' and later: 'When we get away for good I must really take the men in hand and have some good sing-songs.' There might have been some relief when the piano broke away from its moorings in a storm round the Cape of Good Hope, but it was repaired when they put in at Cape Town.

The human conditions were no more predictable than the weather. The cook went crazy and had to be put in irons which he escaped from and threw overboard; a sailor fell from the rigging to the deck and was killed ('Sadness and gloom descended'); there were two fires; and Scott proved a trying commander:

I am supposed to be ready whenever the Captain has a mind to get up anchor . . .

Had a row about last night's fire (some Dundee jute had spontaneously combusted) . . . I expected to be blamed for it and was not disappointed . . .

Through the laconic narratives one can detect friendships forming, irritations growing (when voices were raised the warning 'Girls! Girls!' was often enough to break the tension), and, sometimes, a despondency not even the stiffest upper lip can disguise.

Their last contact with civilisation was in New Zealand where they took on dogs, sheep, provisions and coal, and the ship was invaded by visitors eager to examine the Twentieth-century Argonauts:

All come to gaze at the heroes to be! I say Rats to them all. Heard an amazing story of a young lady being asked why she was coming aboard the ship. She replied that in case of any disaster think how interesting it would be to know that she had actually spoken to one of the officers!! Nice way of looking at things, and not very bright for us.

Within hours of landing in February 1902 they had started to build a hut on shore, and my grandfather had a narrow escape from death by freezing or drowning, or both, when he fell into the sea. They started a routine that would last for two years: sledging in the winter months when the temperatures were higher and the days were long and light, and hibernating during the summer, celebrating Christmas on Midsummer's Day when the night and the day were seamless. 'Absence of sun,' wrote my grandfather, 'has a depressing effect on the best of men.'

The sledge journeys resemble each other more than they differ. The men set out cocky and energetic, dragging an 11 ft sledge with a 7 ft one in tow, six men and (initially) four dogs: Nigger, Bismarck, Paddy and Titch – a music-hall quartet. Their feet sink at the ankles at every step. They steer for Mount Erebus, a still-active volcano, or Mount Terror, undoubtedly appropriately named. Little black silhouettes against the plain white canvas. The dogs fight each other, savagely, picking on the weakest, and their feet start to bleed. 'One or two start to bite their traces, and a good flogging is the only way to teach them not to.' They bay at the moon in chorus, a sound, as Scott said, 'that touches the lowest depths of sadness in this vast desolation'.

The men succumb to exhaustion, frostbite, cramp, and snow blindness. When the weather is calm, the sun stabs the eyes like needles or hot grit, even when wearing wooden goggles with narrow, cross-like slits, and the eyes swell and stream with frozen tears. But then the sledging is easy and the landscape is enchanted: ice cliffs like giants' teeth, glaciers like huge slabs of precious stone, blue and green and glassy and infinitely deep, ice-crystals like a gem-strewn carpet, wonderful optical marvels – double haloes, fog bows, prismatic rings, mock suns, iridescent clouds. And silent, stupendously quiet, but for the 'hush' of the snowcrust settling. Just as quickly the spell dissolves, the wind starts howling, the avalanches growl in the distance, the ice crust cracks with a sound like a volley of pistol shots, and the blizzards blanket their vision with an impenetrable dull white. It is like travelling on the moon, but more desolate and more lonely.

Pitching camp in a blizzard, fumbling for the tent poles and the ground sheet. The slow-motion tedium of taking your clothes off to change into dry ones, ice sticking to your beard, your breath icing, your pipe frozen, your matches damp, your tobacco sodden with snow, your flask of water frozen even though you keep it under your shirt next to your skin; your fingers freeze as you take off your mitts to undo your leggings, and you have to put your mitts on again, and then your leggings are too frozen to undo, the knees hard as bricks, but you have to undo them nonetheless; you take the hay from inside your ski boots and put it next to your body, warm for the morning; you get cramp as you are taking off one pair of your several pairs of long socks, your human-hair night-socks are just pliable enough to put on from being kept close to your body, you wrap yourself in fur, you climb into your sleeping bag, you long for some proper food, something to bite on beside biscuit, you are desperate with tiredness and you are too cold to sleep.

They lived in a time that was hungry for heroes. It was the twilight of the Empire, most of the map of the globe had been coloured pink, and penguins and seals had no territorial rights in the Antarctic. The explorers' scientific purpose was serious and the results impressive, even if this served to mask the less noble motives of the expedition: vanity, self-advertisement, patriotism.

Only the last had gone out of fashion. I am moved by the heroic folly of it all, by the physical courage and endurance, by their resolve never to submit to despair, by their determination, as Tennessee Williams would say, to endure by enduring. It's a practical creed, and my grandfather and his colleagues were practical men whose adventures in the Antarctic I admire no less than Tennessee Williams' exploration of the extremities of the human spirit. You admire what you cannot do yourself.

I grew up surrounded by my grandfather's Polar memorabilia: photos, letters, maps, drawings, water-colours, his goggles, his sealskin gloves, a walrus tooth, some model wooden penguins that he carved himself, and the piano, specially made by Broadwood and still surviving in my basement. I have a beautiful water-colour of Mount Erebus on grey cartridge paper painted by Edward Wilson. Art, he said, is 'reality touched with emotion'. After the expedition a sailor was asked what he specially remembered of the Antarctic – 'Why, the colours,' he said. 'You wouldn't believe them.'

My grandfather stayed in the Navy, rose in rank fast and retired early becoming, with no apparent qualifications, Deputy Commissioner of the Metropolitan Police. He had a short but very happy marriage and he died, in the arms of his wife, of a heart-attack in the ballroom of the Savoy, rehearsing the first waltz for the Police Ball.

My mother was eleven when he died and I don't think she ever recovered from the loss of him. With time my father resented the mute presence of her father and felt indicted by his example. My grandfather's possessions came to seem like threatening totems, relics that she revered and he scorned. He was an only child too, and his father's phantom presence was every bit as strong, every bit as intrusive but far, far more damaging.

IV

My father's family had some faint fibre of a connection with the Victorian passion for exploration. The blood runs rather thinner these days, not only in my family, and if the appetite for adventure hasn't dwindled, the opportunities are finite. Our horizons have contracted and the only unexplored territory now is the territory of the human soul. Instead of gazing out at an unknown continent, we peer inwards to a landscape that is often as mysterious and inaccessible.

I was once asked by a friend, in front of my father, if Lake Eyre in Australia had been named after a relation of mine. 'Oh yes,' I said blithely, 'my great-grandfather's brother.' 'He wasn't,' said my father. 'I think he was,' I said. My father stood up and shouted, with a violence that astonished my friend, but not me, 'Don't tell me about the history of my family!' And I was wrong, of course.

Edward John Eyre, a distant cousin of my paternal great-grand-father, set out from Yorkshire, the son of a parson, to discover the legendary inland sea in Australia. He had arrived at the age of seventeen in New South Wales, where he spent a short time on a sheep farm and as a cowboy, an 'overlander', driving stock from Sydney to Adelaide. He was then twenty-three. As he reflected in his forties, 'I was impelled by an innate feeling of ambition and a desire to distinguish myself in a more honourable and disinterested

way than by mere acquisition of wealth. I was wrong, no doubt –
though I think it is a noble fault to fall into.' Between 1839 and
1841 he opened up huge swathes of uncharted territory.

Fuelled by camp-fire tales of the unrevealed paradise in the
centre of the continent, a giant oasis fed by a vast lake, he set
off from Adelaide in 1840 with a party of six white men, two
aborigines, thirteen horses and forty sheep to 'lift the veil from
the still-unknown and mysterious interior of this vast continent'.
At his departure he was presented with a Union Jack which he
was to plant in the centre of the continent 'as a sign to the savage
that the footstep of civilised man has penetrated so far'.

It was not long before 'civilised' man was humbled by nature;
there was no inland water, no solace, no triumph, only barren
tableland and mirages which bewitched them: 'A vast sheet of
water appeared to intervene between us and the shore . . . the
whole scene partook more of enchantment than reality, and as
the eye wandered over the smooth and unbroken crust of pure
white salt that glazed the basin of the lake . . . the effect was
glittering, and brilliant beyond conception.' It was a monument
to ambition and vain hope.

He was a religious man, a man who interpreted impossible
conditions not as real obstacles but as the workings of destiny,
who stubbornly refused to recognise the furnace-heat of the desert,
the lack of water, the intractable hostility of the terrain as anything
more than challenges to be met and be overcome. He could not
accept nature's mockery of man's insignificance. He was certainly
stubborn, but he was not stupid and therefore not without courage;
a determined romantic, you could say. He was always seeking the
beauty, glorying in the grandiose terror and majesty of exploration.
He did it. I dream about it, and in dreaming know my own
limitations. 'All was uncertainty and conjecture in this region of
magic,' he said after his discovery of the salt lake.

Shortly after I was sent away to boarding school I would
read nothing but POW stories and mountaineering books. The
model escape story was *The Wooden Horse*; prisoners in Stalag

Luft-Something-or-Other dig a tunnel under their gym horse during recreation, and the bags of sand or earth are carried away inside the wooden horse. It was embroidered with the usual seductive detail of forged passports and work permits, cameras made from tins, official stamps and soap, suits made from sacks, uniforms from blankets, and a cast of characters whose weaknesses weren't hard for me to identify with. It fulfilled most of my basic needs: it was frightening, ingenious, difficult, painful, and, above all, true. The penalties for failure were fatal, but the prisoners succeeded in burrowing out of their prison, while I failed to burrow out of mine, even if it was only the tedium and petty oppression of school that I sought to escape from.

Like many bookish schoolboys I read epics of mountain-climbing with an almost pornographic fascination. I loved the vicarious danger and I loved the jargon: bivouacs, abseils, arêtes, crampons, belays, pitons, karabiners, ridges, couloirs, chimneys, slabs and seracs. My favourites were *The White Spider* by Heinrich Harrer, about the climbing of the North face of the Eiger, and *Annapurna* by Maurice Herzog. Both these tales involved terrible physical privations and mental torment. The physical trials included spending the night in a sleeping bag suspended from a vertical cliff by a clip attached to a piton, and losing toes from frostbite on the descent. It wasn't that I was attracted to physical pain – masochism has never held a lure for me – it was the conquest of fear that I found so fascinating. The triumph of the will, I suppose you could say.

My tenuously related ancestor found as bad conditions, or worse, in a journey along the massive natural fortress of the cliffs of the Great Australian Bight that rim the wasteland of the Nullabor Plain. Australia ends suddenly with a sheer drop of hundreds of feet, as if a giant or a god had casually broken off the land and flung it in the sea like a piece of old cheese. After the death of his companion and the defection of his servants, he walked for weeks in the company of a young aborigine boy. They walked nearly a thousand miles. Death was a pleasure kept at bay by the force of an imperative that would have been recognised by my maternal grandfather but not, I think, by me: duty. 'Nothing but a strong sense of duty prevented me from giving way to this pleasing but fatal indulgence. I felt that I could have sat quietly and contentedly, and let the glass of life slide away to its last sand . . .'

I wish I understood this sense of duty; I think that it has vanished along with the other certainties of the last century. I understand duty to friends and to family as a form of love, but not as an abstract, mystical virtue. Perhaps he meant nothing more, or nothing less, than his duty to protect the life of Wylie, the aborigine who had saved his.

There is a terrible paradox in his story. Eyre was one of the few early Australians who thought, and said publicly, that the Europeans should bear in mind that the aborigines regarded them not as legitimate settlers but as invaders and expropriators. After his epic days of exploration he became the Protector and Administrator of the Aborigines in South Australia. He even, for better or worse, educated two aborigine boys in England at his own expense.

He entered the colonial service and in 1865 became Governor of Jamaica. To suppose that you can hold absolute power and not behave like a despot is like supposing you can drink all day and remain sober, and he succumbed to power's fatal lure. The Governor of Jamaica presided as absolute ruler of an island of 16,000 whites and 300,000 blacks. Slavery had ended only in 1833.

Terrible poverty and systematic cruelty provoked a riot led by an inspired revolutionary demagogue. 'It is time for us to help ourselves, skin for skin . . . Every black man must turn out at once, for the oppression is too great.' The riot provoked Eyre into panic: martial law, mass executions, floggings and punitive destruction of property. He was regarded as the saviour of Jamaica by the white settlers, but he was dismissed from office and recalled to London, where his hearing in front of a parliamentary commission provoked riots in the streets. It was a test case for the British

Empire: liberal conscience protested against the thuggish brutality, economic pragmatism defended the necessity of harsh measures to protect British interests. Dickens, Carlyle, John Stuart Mill, Ruskin, Huxley were embroiled in the debate.

There were street riots against Eyre – the London working class identifying with the oppression of the Jamaican blacks; there were street riots in Manchester – the Lancashire working class celebrating the use of force in defence of the cotton and the sugar industry. In the middle dwindled the discoverer of the great Australian salt lake; sour, sad, and bitterly confused. He had, after all, done what he thought was his duty.

There is a River Frome in Southern Australia, which was explored by Edward Eyre. It may have been named after the river that ran through the village in which I grew up. The novelist Sylvia Townsend Warner lived in a Victorian house with a corrugated iron roof at the edge of the River Frome on the way to Frome Vauchurch. I spent countless hours with my sister on the river bank opposite catching minnows and sticklebacks with a net, or tadpoles in a jar, or, later, trying vainly to catch trout with a rod made with a bamboo pole taken from the garden shed. I longed for a world outside our small village where people dealt with the great matters of the world – love and politics and art, I suppose I'd say now – but then anything that would have lifted me out of my social corral. A few feet away was this remarkable apostate revolutionary who lived there all through my childhood. I knew only that she was a 'Communist and a Lesbian', and therefore socially consigned to an oubliette as dark as the one that contained the 'village' boys.

V

My grandfather and my father were proud of what they described as their 'Irish' ancestry, but I've never spoken my surname with much confidence whenever I've been in the West of Ireland. There's an Eyre Square in Galway City, a village of Eyrecourt, and, near by, the picturesque carcase of a large country house. It's roofless, but most of the walls survive, brick here and there peering through the weather-stained white stucco. It was built by John Eyre in the late-seventeenth century when Galway was a remote colonial outpost whose population were mostly Royalist and almost entirely Catholic. John Eyre, an Englishman from Wiltshire, was a Protestant settler, rewarded by Cromwell for services rendered in the Civil War. He had been persuaded of the strength of the Roundhead cause by the King's treatment of his father, who had been punished savagely, even by today's standards, for objecting to an ill-conceived and hastily constructed tax – he was castrated for refusing to pay Ship Money. It was to be drawn from those who lived on the coast to fund the Navy, and was applied with Thatcherite rigour to Giles, who objected, not unreasonably, that Wiltshire was a long way from the sea. His house was plundered by the King's soldiers, he was robbed of £400 and, as a nineteenth-century biography has it, he was 'XXXXed'. Fortunately for the survival of the family he was already the father of eleven children.

The decay of the house, Eyrecourt Castle, looks as though it might be a legacy of the Troubles. The truth of the fate of the estate is less interesting, but its ruin no less deserved. It was a house built for entertainment: a ballroom for dancing, large stables for hunting. It encouraged excess. The pride of the house was the staircase – a double one, carved by Dutch craftsmen and transported from Holland. It is the only part of the interior that remains in existence. It was removed, piece by piece, in the twenties and transported to a museum in Detroit. It was flamboyant and eye-catching, but what really caught the eye of the guest was the inscription over the entrance: WELCOME TO THE HOUSE OF LIBERTY, which was taken so literally in matters of hospitality by successive generations that by the beginning of the eighteenth century the family had exhausted its capital.

A distaste for learning is a family tradition more honoured in the observance than the breach. My father didn't want me to go to university. He wanted me, he said, 'to fuck my way round the world, and learn in the university of life'. I felt wholly unqualified by nature for this, and, as much to defy him as for any other reason, I insisted on breaking the family tradition; I tried, and succeeded, in getting to university. It was the first of many disappointments for him. The son of the founder of the Irish dynasty (another John) had entered Trinity College, Dublin, at the age of sixteen. The following year he was back home, married, with sufficient education to satisfy himself and his father.

In 1760 John Wesley was preaching in the West of Ireland. He brought an unpopular message: no drinking or spirituous liquors, no fighting, or quarrelling or 'doing what we know is not for the glory of God, as putting on of gold or costly apparel'. He observed that the 'ill-breeding' as it showed itself in behaviour was to be found among the 'well-dressed people', and that 'we rode on to Eyrecourt where threatened great things' but, he observed with a Pooterish pun, 'all vanished into air'.

Someone in the family, uncharacteristically, must have concentrated their minds on more substantial matters than spirituous liquors because by the late-eighteenth century the family had acquired 85,000 acres and a peerage. But they reverted to form and a style of living consistent with the family's strengths: 'We hunted all day, danced all night, and strolled about with our lovers.' At least they shared their largesse; they were not absentee landlords, and they lived with an obedience to the household motto which verged on fanaticism. In his old age the noble lord became well known for his hearty appetite and his enthusiasm for cock-fighting. He lived a life described by a contemporary observer that my father read to me with undisguised envy:

> His Lordship's day was so apportioned as to give the afternoon by much the largest share of it, during which, from an early dinner to the hour of rest, he never left his chair, nor did the claret ever quit the table. This did not produce inebriety, for it was sipping rather than drinking that filled up the time, and this mechanical process of gradually moistening the human clay was carried on with very little aid from conversation, for his lordship's companions were not very communicative, and fortunately he was not very curious. He lived in an enviable independence as to reading, and, of course, he had no books. Not one of the windows of his castle was made to open, but luckily he had no liking for fresh air, and the consequence may be better conceived than described.

It was not in the nature of the family, as a biographer commented, to push and strive. The first Lord Eyre died without an heir, the title disappeared and the estate passed to his nephew, Giles, who dedicated himself with wholesale enthusiasm to a life of pleasure:

> To keep game cocks to hunt the Fox
> To drink in punch the Solway
> With debts galore, but fun far more
> Oh! that's 'the man for Galway'.

The 'man for Galway' kept thirty or forty horses for hunting, took no more than two bottles of claret after his dinner to 'drive the gout to his head', and is alleged to have spent £80,000 in bribes during an election – and failed to get elected to parliament. He was approached once by an opponent with a piece of paper in his hand, an offer to retire from the contest if the Squire would sign the declaration. He was confident of his opponent's enviable independence of the skills of reading and writing.

Giles Eyre's lasting claim to fame was his Mastership of the Galway Blazers Hunt. It might be thought that this referred to the pack of hounds, blazing a spirited trail across the countryside in pursuit of the uneatable. Not so. The name was earned by the habit of the Master and his followers putting up at hotels after a hard day's sport and, like a Heavy Metal band high on speed and spirits, setting fire to the hotel. It was perhaps as well for the hoteliers of Galway that overindulgence of all sorts brought the family into debt. Always barely one step ahead of bankruptcy, his son appears to have spent several years in the debtors' prison in Dublin, which does not seem to have hindered his fathering a number of children.

The nephew of one of these children was my great-grandfather, Philip. He was intended by his father for the Church, but bored by the prospect of a life of rural penury, and no doubt tormented by the family's tradition of noisy licentiousness, he ran away from home, enlisted as a private in the South Staffordshire Regiment and left for the Crimea. Here he distinguished himself in battle at the Siege of Sebastopol, was decorated and offered a commission. He was killed thirty years later at the Battle of Kirbekan, leading his regiment as its Colonel. His death was reported in the same week as that of General Gordon, the 'Pacificator' of the Sudan. The *Illustrated London News* reported that he died with these words on his lips: 'I am a dead man. Lord have mercy upon me. God help my poor wife.' It's in the same vein of fiction as the caption that I once saw under a photograph of Indian troops sitting in a trench shortly before Passchendaele: 'They took the fortune of war with the utmost cheerfulness and found considerable solace in the cigarette.'

VI

My great-grandfather's military career cast its shadow over the lives of all his descendants, even my sister and myself. He was clearly a forceful man and I was aware, even as a small child, that his son was cowed by his reputation and diminished by his presence even in death. His portrait hung at the end of the dining-room in my grandfather's house, a stern, patriarchal man, with a large walrus moustache, in full military regalia. The dining-room had dark, dirty, plum-coloured wallpaper, a heavy oak sideboard, a high window that reached from ceiling to floor, and a thick, uneven oak table. My grandfather always sat beneath the portrait of his father and stared malevolently at his son, sitting at the opposite end of the table. He invariably cast a sepulchral silence over meals, punctuated occasionally by a timid dribble of conversation from my sister or from me. During one of these joyless meals she told me that she'd met someone on a train and talked to him. My grandfather slammed his fist on the table, shaking the glasses and the cutlery: 'No one's ever spoken to me in a train, thank *Christ!*'

My parents were never great readers, a novel 'on the go' for my mother from the World Book Club, a military biography for my father, Wellington or Nelson for preference. Beyond that the only required reading was Damon Runyon, P. G. Wodehouse, or *Cold Comfort Farm*. With these exceptions they both preferred the harshness of facts. We were subscribers to the *Reader's Digest*, which ran then, and maybe still does, a regular feature: 'The Most Unforgettable Character I've Ever Met'. My father always said there should be a feature about his father: 'The Most Unpleasant Character I've Ever Met'. When he said that, I never felt he was exaggerating.

Neither Kafka's name, nor his books, were known in our house, but you could get to know Kafka's father through my grandfather. They were brothers in spirit (and in looks) and my father felt about his father as Kafka did of his: 'Often I picture a map of the world and you lying across it. And then it seems as if the only areas open to my life are those that are not covered by you or are out of your reach.' Throughout his life my father struggled to clear a space left unoccupied by his father, and I've made no less an effort in my life. It's a costly operation.

I imagine that my grandfather saw very little of his father, who died when he was eight. He followed his father into the Army but he had a desultory career, and retired early as a major. I asked my father once what his father had done during *his* war, The Great War. 'Sat twenty miles behind the lines at HQ warming his arse on a stove,' he said.

He married my grandmother Joan when they were both in their early twenties, but they were childless for eleven years after their marriage. My father, born in 1916, was their only child. He was very close to his mother and whenever he spoke of her to me his natural reticence about his feelings almost disappeared and a rare tenderness softened his face.

It was always my father's claim that his mother had been killed by his father. I don't think he meant it literally, but I was never quite sure. She died of a stroke when she was fifty-eight, worn out by bullying, long periods of silent disdain followed by eruptions of volcanic severity.

He was even-handed in his brutality and dealt with his son in the same currency. His concept of discipline, at least in practice, was derived from Prussia, or even Sparta. My father was taught to ride before he could walk, tied to a saddle before his legs reached the stirrups. I've seen photographs of him on the back of a plump pony, looking like a pea or a finger puppet. Whatever fear he felt he disguised and it was a lesson he never forgot. Like a wolf child, he was always more at ease with animals than people, and throughout his life could only accept those people who could embrace his love of horses. Try as he might, he found it hard to find fellow feeling with those who had less rigorous childhoods than his own. He was beaten with a riding crop for minor misdemeanours, and when he became a naval cadet at the age of thirteen the consistency and anonymity of the rigid military discipline must have seemed like a benediction. His hair was cut shaved close, within a hair's breadth of his scalp, until he was eighteen; in photographs you can see his skull gleaming through his thin hair. Throughout his adult life he tried to show his independence from his father by growing his hair long, or at least just long enough to make his point but, characteristically, not too long to be unacceptable to convention.

My grandfather lived in a late-eighteenth-century house in North Devon in a small village near Bideford, 'Mau Mau country' my father called it, unfriendly and impenetrable. The house was detached and stood in a few acres of parkland dominated by a huge horse-chestnut tree. On the front of the house two of its large windows were blocked up, legacies of the refusal of a previous owner to pay the Window Tax. It gave the face of the house the look of blindness, as if its eyelids had been sewn together. My grandfather was not rich. He lived on his major's pension and the evidence for this was all too obvious in what he would never have called his lifestyle. If the past is another country, it's one that he had become a native of. He had stopped his personal clock somewhere before the First World War and he dressed always as an Edwardian: narrow-trousered, pale-brown tweed suits, or breeches with puttees and a Norfolk jacket, and always a high-necked, round-edged stiff collar. He was not amused to be told, shortly before he died in the late-fifties, that he was a real Teddy Boy. His hair, though, hardly fitted the bill, shaved Prussian-style close to his scalp like emery paper. If he had a role model it must have been Bismarck, although the suggestion that he resembled a German would have earned a retort: 'I hate the bloody Germans. And the bloody French. And the bloody Italians, for that matter.'

His house was warmed, and I use the word advisedly, by a fire in the dining-room and in his bedroom. There was a firm and unbreakable rule about fires: they were never to be lit before the 1st of October or after the 1st of April. If it snowed on the 2nd of April, so be it; you complained at your peril. He never had electricity installed in the house. All the lighting was done with candles and oil-lamps, all cooking was on a large, black, open, coal-burning range in a kitchen with a flag-stoned floor and a smoke-stained ceiling. The water was pumped in the yard from a well, inhabited by dead cats, rats and frogs. I wish I exaggerated.

The house seemed, to a child's eye, a continent of fearful possibilities: dark, labyrinthine panelled corridors, cellars, creaking floorboards, cupboards that were never opened, rooms that were never entered. The drawing-room was forbidden territory. It was the only room in the house that was light in colour and in feeling, airy and cheerful. We never used it; the grand piano that had been played by my grandmother remained locked, and her collection of musical boxes lay untouched. Her spirit was a palpable presence in the room, and to creep into the room unobserved was to find a calm sanctuary from the potential terrors that lay in the rest of the house. One of these was to be caught by my grandfather using the lavatory at a time when he wanted to use it. This was a common fate of mine, as I could never resist the lure of the only reading matter that was kept there – copies of *Old Moore's Almanac* from years back. The lavatory, an early work by Armitage Ware, was set at the end of a stone-floored tack room, unheated and supplied only with old shredded copies of *The Times* for use as lavatory paper. You'd sit there shivering from fear as much as cold as the door, unadorned by a lock, clattered open and my grandfather stared malignantly: 'How much more bloody time are you going to spend in here?'

In fact there were two lavatories, but the more accessible and, I imagine, more comfortable one was reserved for the use of women. They were not, however, allowed to enter his smoking-room. He may have smoked a pipe but beyond that the purpose of the room was uncertain, or perhaps its purpose was defined simply by its inaccessibility to women. The walls were spread with haphazardly hung rows of sporting and military prints, sepia photographs of Army officers, and brown-paper-covered, dog-eared copies of the Army List dating from before his father's death. Even from the hall the room smelt musty and on the rare occasions that I was allowed in it seemed as welcoming as a monk's cell. It was a melancholy shrine to his past.

There were always household tasks to be set for a child: pumping the water in the yard, cleaning the funnels of the oil-lamps, rubbing the rust off the old iron cutlery, and sometimes, as a treat offered by my grandfather to provoke my father, fetching rough cider from the barrel in the cellar in a heavy, thick glass jug. At the age of six or seven, my sister and I would be encouraged to drink this potent local brew and it never failed to provoke a heady vagueness in us and a full-scale row between them.

I think it was the rows that first attracted my attention to the possibilities of drama, which, unlike fiction, is all about the spaces between the lines. I was fascinated not so much by the obvious entertainment of the inventive streams of violent invective as much as the silences that followed: epic, giant, immense, terrible, and terrifying. Maybe they're magnified by the eyes of childhood, but to me each look had the weight of a hammer blow, each blink a fist. Only the scraping of the cutlery on the plates distracted from the dense absence of words, and broke the almost palpable thickness of the space between them. It was as if the atoms in the air were charged with the anger that they generated, and when my mother offered more fish pie (was it always fish pie?)

the storm would break again, thunderous threats culminating in my mother leaving the room in tears, my sister and I silent as sea anemones, and the two men standing with their fists extended at each other while the shadows made by the flickering oil-lamps danced on the dark ceiling.

Outside his family my grandfather's displays of violence were rare but celebrated. He was bound over to keep the peace several times for assaulting motorists with a horsewhip. He saw himself as a private avenger, keeping the roads free of the alien motor car. When he heard, or more likely scented, an approaching car, he would position his horse across a narrow lane, forcing the driver to stop, and plead to be allowed to pass. Iron-hearted, confirmed in his role as the Scourge of Progress, he resisted all pleas for mercy. The driver would be wound to a pitch of anger and exasperation and get out of his car to move the stubborn object. Then he would be lashed for his insolence, and my grandfather would ride on. 'That'll teach you, you bastard!'

Psychopathic or just plain mad, he was alleged to have many friends, at least as a young man. Like many psychopaths he was fond of practical jokes. He had a cousin who was on the Board of Governors of Bristol Zoo. He rang the zoo pretending to be his cousin and said he was giving a tea-party. He'd be most grateful for the loan of two elephants to be displayed in his garden and was particularly keen that their manure be put to use on his roses. The elephants were delivered on a Saturday afternoon when his cousin was indeed giving a tea-party. He wasn't amused, and I think my grandfather exhausted that friendship as he exhausted the others.

My grandfather had another friend who was a zoologist. He wrote a letter to *The Times* in his friend's name saying that he'd sighted the Loch Ness Monster, a long-necked, long-tailed, pinniped, or fin-footed mammal, some thirty feet in length, which blew like a whale. There was a great deal of excitement, the zoologist was besieged by the press, and his life, at least temporarily, was made hell. This would have given great satisfaction to my grandfather who was an expert in that department.

My mother had a shrewd idea that her life could become hell if she stayed in his house as he'd taken against her on sight and could only be persuaded to speak to her if he wanted some service performed or in order to defame his son. In later years whenever we stayed with him she was banished to the kitchen, or forced to shave his head with fearsome-looking trimmers like crab's claws, but during the War my mother wisely chose to rent a house in a village near him on the estuary of the River Torridge rather than share his house. He was the closest available family: her mother had died soon after the birth of my sister, her uncles had been killed in the previous war, my father was at sea, and London was still being heavily bombed. Her only companion was her nanny, a gaunt, lonely, distant, but kind woman who had been with her since her birth and consequently never quite regarded her as being capable of looking after a child, let alone two. On my mother's honeymoon, spent in the Great Northern Hotel at King's Cross The Day That France Fell, her nanny accompanied her, in a separate room, but my mother was obliged to spend part of the night with her chaperone. Unsurprisingly, my mother always seemed faintly daunted by her, and asserted her rights of access to us as if she lacked the natural conviction in them. My sister and I grew up between the two of them, never quite certain whose authority to defer to.

I was born on a Sunday in March 1943. I was once persuaded to visit a foot-reader, or 'reflexologist' as he called himself. He told me I had been born late and that my mother had been unhappy during my pregnancy. The rest of your life, he said, you will be trying to make up for your late entry into the world; your mother didn't want to let you go. As it happened, it was true what he said. I was late, she was unhappy, and I don't think she did ever want to let me go. She missed my father, and it was six months before he saw me. For a few months she kept a diary of my growth, interspersed with her visits, announced at very short notice, to Derry, or Dover, or Plymouth. On these short visits she had 'a marvellous time', 'a heavenly weekend', 'a thrilling time'. When my father had his first sighting of his son it was said by my mother to be favourable.

My grandfather wrote that he was pleased to hear of the safe arrival of 'the gift from God' (I assume that was heavy irony). 'Some day soon I will give you my considered opinion of your effort.' I have no idea what his considered opinion was but it may well have been reflected in his instruction that I was to be christened 'Richard Fitzrichard', or, as I understand it, bastard son of Richard. Fortunately, the vicar was deaf and christened me 'Richard . . . er, just Richard'. A small act of mercy.

We lived in North Devon until the end of the War, and returned there annually on a pilgrimage that was penitential, at least for my father. It wasn't so for me. I liked the strangeness of it all; it was like time-travelling. I was fascinated by my grandfather and his house, and during the long hot summer days we'd often go back to Instow where we'd lie on the beach looking across the Torridge to Appledore waiting until low tide to walk across the estuary to go shrimping in the pools.

It was on one of these shrimping expeditions that I had my first sexual experience. We'd had a picnic on the beach, a lot of drink for the grown-ups, a lot of noise. I remember my mother telling everyone not to go swimming, they'd had too much to drink. As a child, she said, she'd been in Deauville and seen the town band go swimming after a huge, drunken lunch; they'd staggered across the flat sand into the sea, and several failed to return, drowned. But the tide was too low to swim and we all trooped off to the shrimping pools. I'd watched slyly earlier as a friend of my mother's changed out of her wet bathing suit into her dress. Now she slipped on the wet sand and fell back into a pool with a shriek of laughter. She wrung out her dress, and, as she did so, once again observed by me, revealed what I already knew – she wore no knickers. She caught my eye and smiled, a smile of sweet complicity.

Throughout those summers I lived with a lightness of spirit, shoeless, with a minimum of clothes. Occasionally I would be sunburnt, but even that had its compensations. Going up to my room with the green-painted cupboard up the narrow back staircase, carrying a Wee Willie Winkie candle, to lie on my bed while my mother rubbed Calomine lotion on my back and then read *Struwwelpeter* to me, the only children's book in the house. But not even the tales of chopping off fingers and eating babies destroyed the pleasure of hearing my mother's voice as the soothing pink lotion on my back dried like cracked clay.

My grandfather had a mistress. She was a widow, who lived in the village, and was occasionally glimpsed by me on one of my reconnoitres of forbidden territory. I'd be drawn by the sound of hushed voices and doors which mysteriously closed as I approached. I once went into the dining-room as his friend, the exotically named Mrs de Las Casas, was being ushered out rather indecorously over the low sill of the window. It was a compulsory fiction that the affair was not taking place, but her presence made itself felt at second hand: 'My friend, Mrs de Las Casas, says . . .' while my father muttered, 'I don't give a bugger what your friend Mrs de Las Casas says.'

She was revealed in her true colours at my grandfather's funeral, an occasion which my father said was no less welcome for having been so long awaited. 'It just goes to show that there's a God,' he said. He sat at the front of the church during the funeral and at one point, being aware of someone getting up behind him, he looked round and saw Mrs de Las Casas leaving the church carrying a large shopping bag. His curiosity got the better of his filial affection without much difficulty and he followed her. She crossed the road and went into my grandfather's house, through the back door, down the dark corridor from the kitchen to the hall, and into the dining-room. For a few moments my father waited, listening to a shuffling, chinking sound. When he went into the room, she turned, frozen, her hands full of silver cutlery. 'He always wanted me to have this,' she said defiantly.

My grandfather's sole concession to the twentieth century was a large radio, or rather, 'wireless', which was powered by a large accumulator. Its use was permitted only twice a day: *The Nine o'Clock News* in the morning, and *The Nine o'Clock News* at night. Parsimonious as this was, I always loved sitting round the wireless, focusing on the art deco panel in front of the loudspeaker, and the portentous, dinner-jacketed voice of the news-reader. I liked the ritual and the forced family gathering.

I was away at school when my grandfather died. I'd persuaded my father that he should give me a radio to replace my crystal set and when they came to see me they were going to bring it. But their visit was cancelled: 'Your grandfather has died and your parents won't be able to bring your wireless. I expect you're sorry about that.' I was, but I was sorrier still that Grandpa had died. I wasn't sure why. Something had gone from my life, I wasn't sure what.

VII

We all grow up in the same way, more or less;
Life is not known to give away her presents;
She only swaps.

> – W. H. Auden, 'Letter to Lord Byron'

The absent father is a literary commonplace drawn from the commonplace of life. My father's generation had yet to become self-conscious about the role of the father, or willing to articulate the frustration of the mother, and I'm none too certain that he would have stayed at home if he'd had the choice. Like many of his generation, he was emancipated by his life in the Navy, and although it was undeniably dangerous to be at Dunkirk, and hell to be on a convoy in the Baltic, there was a licence for him to see the world during and after the War, and an implicit licence for the sort of behaviour dictated by the thrill of beating death: a licence for licence.

Until I was eight I have only intermittent memories of my father but I do remember trying to get him to teach me to swim. There was a picnic, friends and their children, and food and drink spread out on the grass of a water-meadow beside a large weir pool, sheltered on the other side by white willows and osiers. There was the smell of an English summer, fresh river water, grass and the faint scent of cowshit on the breeze. The weir itself had several floodgates which could be wound up and down according to the level of the water, and a flat area beneath the gates where the water collected before spilling into the river below. I longed to be able to swim from the weir to the shore, a distance of perhaps fifty feet.

I tried to distract my father. He was engaged on an apparently endless anecdote about how he had to put his hand down a woman's dress to extricate a hearing-aid that had fallen down the front, and then shown a couple to the coal-hole who 'couldn't wait to do it'. I waited until the end of the story and asked him to teach me to swim. 'If you swim from the weir to the bank,' he said, 'I'll give you ten shillings,' and he brandished a note. Greed overcame fear and I ran to the weir. I confidently assumed that he wouldn't be watching, secured a large piece of timber which supported my weight, and paddled like a sodden dog to the shore. As I lay in the water panting, preparing to collect my reward, a condom floated towards me. I held up my find. 'What's this? What's this?' I yelled in the face of a blast of laughter. 'It's a trap for catching eels,' said my father without pause and that was the extent of his swimming tuition, and, for that matter, sexual education. I was expected to acquire knowledge by osmosis.

Years later I was on the beach at Southsea with my mother. She fell asleep, and while she slept I was convinced that I could learn to swim by the power of positive thought. I strode out into the sea towards my sister, who was an able swimmer. I was soon out of my depth and unaccountably my flailing arm movements failed to keep my head above water, and I clung to my sister's neck, dragging the two of us downwards. The role I'd inadvertently given my sister was typical: she was supporting me. When I asked her years later if she remembered this episode I remembered only my part. I'd forgotten, typically again, that I'd almost dragged her down with me. We were saved from drowning by a prompt spectator and I was carried, before the fascinated gaze of the entire beach, back to my sleeping mother. She woke to see a bluish child deposited at her feet. In gratitude she gave my saviour £5; even in my bleary, sodden, tear-clouded state I can remember the look of grateful surprise as he took the large white note, and I thought: Oh, that's what I'm worth. I learnt to swim for free a few years later.

As a young girl my mother had been a keen swimmer, a golfer, a skier, even a rider, but with time and marriage these enthusiasms dropped away. My parents' real passion was for parties, and I was conscripted reluctantly into these as a truculent waiter, ferrying drinks to guests who would have preferred a direct connection with the bottle. They seemed to have discovered the secret of circular breathing, talking seamlessly, without the need to pause to take in drink or air. From the child's-eye view I saw their huge chests as mere containers for liquid and their braying voices as mere devices for making noise. If they spoke to me I was paralysed by shyness, and if I spoke to them it would be to experiment with the code of address in which my father had instructed me: all male adults (of a certain class) were to be called 'sir'. My levelling instincts rebelled and I took a malicious delight in public refusal in spite of the inevitable punishment, often being chased round the garden to evade the hard slap of my father's hand and the incarceration in my room, where I steamed for hours with righteous indignation.

My father never lost the habit of treating parties as if the War had cast the mould for 'a good thrash', and anything less would be a betrayal of the past. He had a rapacious attitude to pleasure, underpinned by a kind of urgency. His creed, borrowed perhaps from the 'House of Liberty' of his profligate ancestor, was this: 'Enough is too little, too much is enough.' If the Suez Canal was said to flow through the drawing-room of Anthony Eden during the Suez crisis, rivers of gin seemed to flow through ours. It may have been a legacy of the War years, or it may have been a rebellion against an abstemious childhood, but it persisted almost until his death. He had a contagious energy, and, when his insistent enjoyment joined with my mother's exuberance, they were a hard couple to resist. They never seemed more themselves and more together than when they were on the opposite sides of a room hosting a party, radiating a mutual warmth and defying the guests not to enjoy themselves. Their charm was not so much infectious as guileless, but for me at least, it was a sort of tyranny of fun – there seemed no room for dissent.

There's a cartoon that people often send to me on first nights, when I put my head on the professional block: 'How to Behave at a Preview'. A couple stand at an art exhibition, the man's elbow is poised on an imagined mantelpiece, a glass in his hand, the woman is seated below him. HE: 'This is my masterpiece – hand and glass locked in a tension of opposites.' SHE: 'Don't be a wally, Nigel – people will hear you!' The context clouds the picture. My parents would have been as likely to be seen at a Nubian fertility dance as at an art exhibition, but their masterpiece was indisputably hand and glass locked for a lifetime in a tension of opposites.

If they enjoyed themselves with a passionate intensity, when they fought it was no less intense. I had a miniature bricklaying set, a sort of crude precursor of Lego, tiny terracotta bricks, stuck together with a sort of soluble mortar. I had spent a day building a bungalow, pitched roof and bow windows, which I carried before me down the stairs like a burning Christmas pudding to display to my parents and bask in their admiration. As I opened the door our white Bakelite radio, propelled by my father, flew across the room towards my mother and seemed to stick to the wall: valves, wires, condensers, resistors, transformers, all slipping slowly down the wall like entrails or jelly. Violence freezes the senses. It's often shown on film in slow motion and it seems meretricious. Yet there really are two simultaneous timescales, the real and the perceived, the objective and the subjective. I was once beaten up, in Singapore. I can remember every moment of the impact as if it had been minutely catalogued, yet it was over, with startling force, in a matter of seconds. The radio seemed to take the rest of my childhood to drift down the wall.

Like most children of my class I was sent to boarding school when I was eight, and progressed, according to the custom of the tribe, from prep school to public school. Evelyn Waugh's much celebrated view of the public school now has the status of a revealed truth: 'Anyone who has been to an English public school will always feel comparatively at home in prison. It is the people brought up in the gay intimacy of the slums . . . who find prison so soul-destroying.' It's an observation that's often quoted in a self-congratulatory fashion by those who'd have you believe that their education has done them no harm and, as if to prove the proposition, they intend to send their sons to endure the same treatment. Leaving aside Waugh's fantasies about the 'gay intimacy of the slums', there is much truth in the comparison between public school and prison. Both institutions harbour people who would rather not be there, both apply a senseless discipline in the name of self-improvement, both insist on class solidarity, both pay lip-service to remedial education, both encourage the suppression of natural feelings, and both encourage an orthodoxy of homosexuality.

At least prisons have a rational justification for their existence; the justification for the seminaries of the English middle class is harder to find, but its consequences are all too visible. The custom of sending children to boarding schools at the age of eight has an air of calculated cruelty that does not have the excuse of ignorance or helplessness. It is no exaggeration to say that the moment I was left alone in late September on a playing field in Hampshire as my parents drove away inspired a pain and resentment that the wisdom or forgiveness of hindsight hasn't diminished. Perhaps I was more than usually thin-skinned, but I knew then as I listened to the cawing of the rooks and gazed at the bleak faces of my fellow new boys, all struggling to conceal their misery, that it was a high price to pay. To be taught to survive is one thing, to be taught that it is unwise, unmanly and unsafe to share your feelings is quite another. This is the fate of English Middle-Class Man.

No one has written with more eloquence of the English middle-class educational system than Orwell, and yet, as if unable to eradicate his tribal loyalties, he obliged his own (adopted) son to endure the same rites of passage that he so despised. Perhaps he wanted his son to learn the same lesson he had to learn, as a child poorer than the other children: 'A child conscious of poverty will suffer snobbish agonies such as a grown-up person can scarcely even imagine.' Through suffering he would learn; a political education, but at what cost? More often, fathers who have suffered themselves will, like homeopathy, apply a little of the same treatment to their children as if to assuage their own memories, or simply to convince themselves it was all for their good. It made men of them. More pathetic still is the spectacle of those who didn't have the dubious benefits of this education, craving it for their own children as the essential qualification for membership of the club that they've been taught, by the existing members, is essential for their social advancement. Easy enough for me to say, of course, as a member of the club.

We are a deeply conservative, and a deeply religious people. The only possible explanation that I can see for the survival of, and deference to, the Monarchy, the House of Lords, the Honours system, the British Constitution (or lack of it), is that we have a kind of mystical faith in our systems and institutions that is not susceptible to reasoned analysis and debate. They are regarded, in a real sense, as sacred. Our feelings are passionately religious – no less so than Islam – and are all the more powerful for not being acknowledged as such; it is, after all, an *English* religion. The clock was stopped when the mortality of the Empire was perceived and progress was frozen somewhere around the Jubilee in 1897. It's not a coincidence that the form of many of our 'time-honoured' pageants and rituals was conceived by committees in Queen Victoria's reign in the wake of Disraeli's coinage of the title 'Empress of India'. They are as synthetic as the annual gathering of the Druids on Primrose Hill to celebrate the Summer Solstice. We call congenitally retarded children, the sufferers from Down's Syndrome, 'mongols'. In Japan they call them 'Britons'.

To judge by the standards of the voluminous literature of the English middle-class education, my prep school was typical, and

I was happy enough there. There were some excellent teachers: an American student who loved to talk about the French Revolution – I can still remember his rhapsodic description of the importance of the Gabelle, the tax on salt, as a trigger to the Revolution; a Latin teacher with one eye, tall as a poplar tree, severe but kindly; an ex-Commando major who had lost his leg in Normandy and used his tin leg to gain our attention, banging it with his stick, or, in extremity, hurling the same stick like a lance to hit a recalcitrant pupil with the rubber end right between the eyes. He loved reading aloud and had a wonderfully alluring voice, like an English Spencer Tracy, and he gave us, over four or five lessons, the whole of Matthew Arnold's epic narrative poem about the Norse Gods, *Balder Dead*. It was dense, vivid, and unflaggingly exciting. I looked at it again the other day and realised what an alchemist my teacher had been. But the reading that converted me to the power of descriptive writing was Hemingway's *The Old Man and the Sea*. In the classroom we unhesitatingly identified the Old Man with the teacher, our old man, and when he finished the story there was a silence that could have been carved into a monument. The Major took an interest in me, thought that I had a talent for acting, and wrote a play for me – *The Man Who Won the Pools*, and I was that man. We performed it after the school prize-giving, to applause that intoxicated me and corrupted me irrevocably.

His interest in me was of a different sort to Uncle Willie who taught French, and kneaded one's legs just above the knee, and to the Headmaster who weighed us twice a term in our underpants and then confirmed his measurements by sitting us on his knee and bouncing us up and down in a fairly unscientific fashion. We were cynically aware of the Headmaster's follies, but not cynical enough to encourage them. Sex seemed innocent enough and we discovered the delights of masturbation, lying in small huts we constructed in the woods out of branches and warm hay after smoking pipes turned on the lathe in the woodwork shop and stuffed with the tobacco from discarded cigarette ends.

It was a school mostly for the sons of naval officers, and its maritime bias was expressed in a large flagpole, like a mast, which stood in the forecourt. Every morning the Union Jack and the flags for four admirals who had given their names to the 'houses' at the school were raised by the boys. It was a much envied privilege, and I count among the more useful things I learnt at school the knowledge of how to roll a flag, run it up a pole, and unfurl it on cue.

Weekends always had a particular flavour, part desolation and part exhilaration. It was a mixed blessing to have a visit from one's parents – the strain of having to spend time with comparative strangers and one's anxious awareness of their efforts to be entertaining were at war with the pleasures of remaining at school. A melancholy walk on the esplanade at Southsea followed by a meal spent with half an eye on the clock could hardly be preferable to being left to enjoy the film on Saturday night – a short, often a *Ma and Pa Kettle*, followed by a feature, perhaps *King Solomon's Mines*, an Ealing comedy, a George Formby, or, exceptionally, a bona fide American movie.

And on Sunday nights anarchy ruled. There never seemed any evidence of staff after the church service and the meal on Sunday evenings, and this invisibility enabled a wild, atavistic display of violence to occur. The whisper went round the school: 'Chain He in the gym,' and by seven o'clock about a hundred boys had collected. One was chosen 'He' and formed a chain which grew and swung and swept the length of the large echoing gymnasium gathering its victims in its jaws. To be one of the last to be caught was to know real excitement and real fear: the sight and sound of nearly a hundred small boys drunk with infectious savagery, screaming with demonic glee, thundering towards me with plimsolls thudding like hooves on the springy floor lives with me still. I loved the feeling of fear as much as the feeling of power.

My public school was exceptional only in that it had a more stubborn hold on the nineteenth century than others at the time, and that I was finally expelled from it – for a mixture of boredom, rebelliousness, exasperation on their part and sheer bloody-mindedness on mine. In my last year I'd engineered a kind of no man's land between science subjects and English. I convinced the science teachers that I was occupied with English, and the English teacher vice versa, and I filled the ensuing vacuum by breeding a contagious discontent and editing the school magazine. Its satirical tone was ahead of its time, but that was all that there was to recommend it under my editorial hand. A stray copy of the proofs reached the Headmaster's eyes; the issue was plucked from the presses and an apparatchik was installed as a substitute editor. The incident coincided with a trip that I made to a sixth-form conference at Watford Grammar School. Suitably dressed in black shirt, white tie, drainpipe trousers and winklepicker shoes, I made my way to the station. 'Where are you going?' said the school chaplain. He spoke mildly, in fact somewhat in the tone of a man musing on his text for next Sunday's sermon, but my fuse blew. I told him it was no business of his where I was going, caught the train, and by the time I returned I was the only person in the school who didn't realise that my half-life was over. Shortly afterwards, when I was eighteen, I became a barman. I revealed to a customer that I'd been expelled from school. 'For rogering behind the pavilion,' he said, and I couldn't satisfy him with the truth.

When I was expelled I was confronted by the Headmaster. He told me that I would regret leaving under these circumstances all my life, and cited the change of heart of Alec Waugh, Evelyn's brother, who had been expelled some forty-five years earlier for writing a novel about the school that indicated that homosexuality and bullying were the most conspicuous educational disciplines on offer. It didn't seem like fiction to me. The Headmaster was still pretty steamed up about it, but the point he made was this: 'Alec Waugh lives abroad now and he returns to this country twice a year. The first occasion is the Lord's Test, and the second occasion is the Old Shirburnian's Dinner. I think there's a lesson to be learned there, don't you agree?'

I didn't.

*

I don't think the parting of the ways with my father was entirely my fault – but then I don't think it was entirely his. When I was nine he was sent to South-East Asia, or, as he called it, and it seemed accurate enough to me, 'The Far East'. He was away for over two years and he became a series of X's on a postcard: his cabin on a P and O liner, the bridge of his ship – the destroyer *HMS Consort*, the Peak in Hong Kong, the old palace of the Rajah Brooke's in Sarawak. The postcards got less frequent, the X's disappeared, and I was left with the Esplanade in Macao, the City of Tokyo, the Island of Formosa, and a remoteness as wide as three continents.

We waited for several hours on a cold night at Stansted Airport to meet him on his return. Somehow I expected to see him in uniform, the sharply pressed white-uniform shorts that he wore in the bleached black-and-white photographs he had sent us. I was disappointed by the man I met, undoubtedly my father, but less big, less romantic, and, above all, less welcoming than I had hoped. Perhaps I didn't make it easy for him, but instead of kissing me as he had when he left, he patted me on the shoulder, perhaps with awe: I was no longer the child he had left behind.

The next night we went out to dinner at Quaglino's – a supper club whose great days belonged to a past when nightingales sang in Berkeley Square. I sat next to my father feeling somehow as if I'd won the evening as a prize in a competition. Stirring the conversational pot my father asked me how my riding was going. To him it was an accomplishment as casual, and as necessary, as tying your shoelaces.

'I don't . . . er . . . much like riding,' I said, staring at my plate. He snapped back without hesitation. 'That's because you're no bloody good at it.'

The truth, which amounted to the same thing in his eyes, was that I was frightened of it. I was naturally physically quite timid, and as far as horses were concerned my timidity had been reinforced by breaking my arm while trying to mount a pony bareback like

51

Tonto, and by seeing my sister dragged by a bolting horse along a gravel path. But my fear drove him away as surely as if I'd declared that I had cholera.

I sat in silence for the rest of the meal and when we returned to the Cadogan Hotel, I was a little older and a lot sadder. Many people think of Oscar Wilde's arrest when they pass the Cadogan Hotel. I think of the night my father gave up on me. What we have to admit is that the failures are not only those of other people; they are our own. If he was punishing me for failing to live up to his expectations, I was doing the same to him. And I should not assume that it cost him less than it cost me.

'There are only two classes of good society in England: the equestrian classes and the neurotic classes. It isn't mere convention: everyone can see that the people who hunt are the right people and the people who don't are the wrong ones,' says Shaw in *Heartbreak House*. I'd declared myself a member of the neurotic classes, but for several years I failed to concede the divide and made strenuous attempts to redeem myself in my father's eyes, before conceding the impossibility and resigning myself to years of armed truce. When I was appointed Director of the National Theatre there was a characteristically inaccurate item in the *Evening Standard* about how I was seeking to 'ascend into the squirearchy' by joining the hunting fraternity, 'turning from red to pink'. They weren't to know the painful irony of their fiction. They printed a correction from my father: 'Someone's been pulling your whizzer,' he said. 'My son is grown up and I don't dictate to him whether he should go hunting, or drink a bottle a day, or have three women a week.' That at least had the unmistakable tone of his voice and what he said of himself was true, but not through want of trying.

My mother too belonged to the neurotic classes, and she compensated for her alienation with an engaging and restless energy which defied nature in a form of perpetual motion. She was an organiser with an idiosyncratic but systematic method of reducing chaos to order: list followed list as she marshalled her resources with the flair of a natural general. It wasn't unusual to be asked at supper what you wanted for breakfast, lunch *and* dinner the next day, or to find her planning her Christmas shopping in June. Her cooking was self-taught and by any standards touched with genius; the secret of the perfect meringue has died with her. She was a dedicated, knowledgeable and enthusiastic gardener who spoke of plants by their Latin names with the confident certainty of an expert.

My father retired from the Navy in his early-forties when I was twelve. He became a farmer. In spite of the fact that for years he was anything but a dilettante, he liked to be referred to as a 'gentleman farmer'. For a while my mother ran a catering business, cooking for large, sometimes huge gatherings, and my father must have thought that they were coming perilously near to being 'trade'. She was happy in her work, he was happy in his, and even, for a while, so was I.

His farm was a mile and a half from our house by foot – over the railway line, up the steep hill scarred by lynchets from the Bronze Age, and into the next valley. The farm was hilly chalkland, covered with bracken and rabbit holes. I loved helping him clear thorn bushes, fields of thistles, build fences, and mend barns. He transformed this unpromising land into something that was, for a while, almost profitable: there were beef cattle, corn, even turkey for two seasons. It's a Nature Conservancy Reserve now, and has reverted back to its natural wildness; it's home to species of wild orchids and a rare butterfly.

I once saved his life. He pierced an artery in his arm on barbed wire and I made a tourniquet from his shirt. I wasn't generally as useful but I was tolerated, and at harvest-time made to feel that I was doing real work. I drove the tractor pulling the baler, even sometimes the combine-harvester. For a few years I was too small to lift straw bales on to the trailer, but I was never happier than when I was allowed to stack them and sit on top as we drove back to the barn with the sun setting and the stacked piles of straw rolling like a galleon in a heavy sea.

At heart my mother was a town girl, but she made spirited attempts to counter this impression. She was never too much worried by the Muscovy ducks wandering into the kitchen from the garden, or Rex the Ram following them and drinking out of the dogs' water bowl. But her most conspicuous identification with the farm was her adoption of our bull. He was a hornless Hereford, brown-and-white, who she bottle-fed as a calf, and watched over in our orchard as he grew into a creature of awesome size. She was very fond of him and she had very mixed feelings as we walked him one day up the hill to present him to his wives.

My father started to race horses, or, to be more accurate, he raced his one horse 'over the jumps' and I tried to share his sport vicariously. I visited most of the National Hunt courses in the South of England, trailing after him, trying to convince him that, although of the neurotic classes, I was still acceptable in a man's world. He was never fooled, and neither was I, but I enjoyed the life on the courses and I still do. Out in front over the fences, he was a hero: black-and-yellow quartered jersey, quartered cap, thundering, thumping, crashing through the fences. Falling sometimes, his shoulder dislocated, he would bellow at the St John's Ambulancemen, 'Leave me, don't touch me,' crawl on to a stretcher, and I'd follow him to the doctor who pushed his shoulder into its socket as if he was forcing a leg into the seat of a chair.

There's something comforting about race-tracks. They're always the same: the camelhair coats, the British warms, the anoraks and the Barbors; the thick, rubberised Burberry raincoats of the trainers, bookies in sheepskins and Max Miller trilbies; large, check Viyella shirts, hairy ties, flat-brimmed, grey-brown felt hats over piggy, Gainsborough-pink round faces; ageless aristocrats with light-brown, velvet-collared overcoats; dark-brown, furled-brim trilbies perched like apostrophes on chinless heads of under-employed Army officers, the sharper, more jaunty trilbies of the touts or the trainers, the bowlers of the race-course officials, the plaids, the checks, the tweeds, the whisky, the gin, the beer, the beer, and the beer, and the piss splashing back on your feet from the wall of a galvanised-iron urinal; the faces marinated in alcohol and broiled in rain and strong winds; the gorblimey caps of the stable boys, the pony-tails of the girls; the shield-shaped tags that admit you to the paddock, the display ring, the holy of holies, where you stand self-consciously brushing shoulders with the riders, trainers, owners, officials; and the horses sleek, and tense, and beautiful, gaped at by the knowing, cynical and unimpressed crowd pressing at the rails; bulky binoculars, wads of notes, torn betting slips, tote tickets, thick ham sandwiches. And the talk, the crack, literally over my head, of the form, the going, the SP, the tips: 'from the horse's mouth', 'he's a goer', 'he won't run'; 'he's a donkey', 'know what I mean?'; the villains, the bent jockeys, the real gents – Fred Winter, made in heaven; and the courses that still ring like a catechism for me: Wincanton, Newton Abbot, Plumpton, Chepstow, Cheltenham, Exeter, Taunton, and Fonthill. There's a kind of day in February or early March that always makes me think of the races: scudding clouds, strong winds, fugitive glimpses of pale sun, a downpour, then a bright, glistening sunlight that seems to put a polish on everything, followed by a sunset the colour of a dying bruise.

Apart from riding, my father's main enthusiasms were drink and sex; often, if we were to believe the stories, all three were combined on the hunting field. He had an astonishing constitution for drink. Maybe it was the war-time training, or maybe it was the pint of water that he drank every night before sleep, but he rarely showed signs of damage the next day. He found it hard to understand a teetotaller, and regarded a reluctance to get drunk as a weakness of character. He had an equally forceful attitude to sex. He was attractive to women and was acquisitive. His approach was frank and, I hope, more sensitive than his public performance as the wenching squire – all slap, pinch and tickle. His conquests, real or imagined, and those of my mother, were the seed-corn of his banter, and, if my mother was embarrassed by this, that suited his comic turn. He made much mileage out of an incident at our village railway station: he was stepping out of the London train as my mother's lover was returning to London on the opposite platform. I never tested this tale against the railway time-table; it was the status of folklore, and I preferred it that way. Only later did I learn the true extent of their mutual infidelities. My father may have encouraged my mother to imitate him, but there was no disguising his shock when he discovered a list of my mother's lovers, real or imagined, that she had kept in her dressing-table. I'm sure then that he wished that he had known nothing, and I, of course, wished the same for myself.

He encouraged me to think that conquest was all, invoking a sort of competitive promiscuity, which, far from emancipating me, made me feel anxious and inadequate for failing to fulfil his implicit quota. I was never sure where the banter ended and reality began. We did not speak of love, or happiness, or even of pain.

It was difficult to bring my girlfriends near him without passing through a drizzle of teasing or worse. He would either attempt to seduce them (once, to my everlasting bitterness, successfully), or he would frighten them off with his robust wit. He could be counted on to greet a new girlfriend with the refrain: 'Time is short and we must seize/ Those pleasures found above the knees,' and then he'd laugh with a goatish snort at my pained embarrassment.

In matters of sex he was impatient with euphemism. He despised Hardy's novels for that reason. I tried to get him to read *Tess of the d'Urbervilles*, not least because much of it is set within miles of where we lived. 'Why doesn't he say they do it, when they do it?' He was a man who would call a spade a spade. Or to be more accurate, a bloody spade. Or to be more truthful, a fucking spade. Only now can I see the small boy in the grown man, bullied and beaten by his father into a resolve to show no softness in public, least of all to his son.

Am I being fair to him? He had great energy, a sharp wit, Rabelaisian inventiveness, great charm when he chose to apply it, and a rare tenderness, even if it was often reserved for animals, or for my sister, whose view of him was almost the polar opposite of mine. He caricatured his father to me, and perhaps I'm doing the same to him. Perhaps all of us do that of our parents; the reality is too complex. I paint my mother too white, my father too black. The real picture is too shaded with guilt, love, hatred, resentment, and wish for approval to be rendered accurately. I am standing too close to the canvas.

As we grew apart my mother became an uneasy negotiator, her loyalties confused. At school I distilled my resentment of my father into a kind of ideology that lay somewhere between anarchy and communism. My cardinal principle was to oppose whatever my father stood for. 'The Tories are it; the others are just politicians,' he said, and I found no difficulty turning that adage on its head. I clamoured for attention, and found it in acting. The fact that it interested my father as much as the economy of Albania made it all the more attractive. When my father said that he didn't want me to go to university, that it was a waste of time, it was an act of defiance to try. I wanted to colonise a world that he hadn't invaded.

I never spoke to my mother much about all this. She was modest about her intellect and often hesitant about stepping on uncertain ground, she represented herself as less clever than she was. She always felt intellectually inferior to my father, and he endorsed her inadequacy. At first it was playful teasing; then it hardened by use into a sort of systematic bullying.

My father never came to see my work in the theatre, but, on one or two occasions, my mother did. She came to see *Comedians* in London and we went to dinner afterwards. She didn't often come to London and she was quite different when we were alone. No longer parroting my father's opinions or his tone of voice, she was something like herself, soft, tentative, and instinctive.

She was trying to understand who I was, and I was doing the same with her. She told me that she wasn't happy, she hinted at trouble with my father, but she was not disloyal. She asked gently about my own life, and we spoke about the play, and about the central character: a violent, almost psychopathic, romantic, dispossessed working-class boy, consumed by a raging despair. 'I'd never realised how much you hated your school. I'm sorry, I should have asked,' she said.

In one sense we never grow up. To our parents we are always children and we view their marriage through the eyes of a child. It is hard enough to penetrate the façade of any marriage; we never have the necessary evidence to condemn or acquit, to allocate blame or innocence. Some marriages sustain for years an inscrutable face to the world, then collapse with a terrible suddenness which unnerves friends who had counted them as the fixed point in their moral and social constellation. Other marriages, fuelled by constant public attritional warfare, miraculously survive – the more secure perhaps for never having been perceived as exemplary. The evidence for our parents' marriage is always hopelessly tainted by our own prejudice and wishful thinking. We long to believe that the happiness we saw was not superficial, assumed for our benefit, and that the pain was a temporary accident of circumstance. In later years it was apparent to anyone, even to their children, that my parents' marriage had reached a bitter stalemate.

But when my parents married they were very much in love. I don't say this as a sentimental attempt to salvage a sunny beginning from a story that became increasingly dark. I know it to be true. I was going through their papers after my father died, trying to sift what should be saved, what should be discarded. It was like an archaeological dig: layer after layer of dust, photographs, chequebooks, bank statements, Christmas cards, solicitors' letters, mortgages, press cuttings, magazines, the whole detritus of their lives impacted like peat in layer after disordered layer. Like the burn-marks on stones, the papers gave evidence to the fact that they had *lived* but, with the exception of some photographs, not *how* they had lived. And the photographs told little to the archaeologist: it was always summer, these people were always smiling, *ergo* they were always happy. But among the hundreds, perhaps thousands of photographs, there was not a single picture of a family group: mother, father, son and daughter. It's unscientific to me, but I'm reluctant to draw conclusions.

The Rosetta Stone was a small, heavy brown-leather suitcase, full of letters, elastic-banded bundles of them, hundreds, perhaps thousands, mostly on blue air mail paper: 'AIR MAIL LETTER CARD USE OF HM FORCES ONLY.' I stared at the letters, certain that I was never meant to see them. I recognised my father's handwriting and tentatively withdrew a letter. I read only enough to blush at the invasion of their privacy. For a long time the suitcase was there as a *memento mori*, a relic that could only be revered.

The day after my mother died I realised I was on my own, free at last of the influence of both my parents. It was what I thought I'd always wanted, and yet I felt utterly bereft. I felt a hopeless desire to get in touch with my mother, talk to her, touch her. I was free of all restraint and I opened the suitcase full of my father's letters.

It's always a mistake to read things that are not intended for one's eyes – a school report, an assessment, a reference, a letter. These were no exception. They were lustful, bawdy, playful, loving, blunt, larded with a profusion of inventive endearments, and a cascading litany of sexual address that made me smile, and blush, and smart, and drop large tears on to the sheaves of pale-blue envelopes. I was glad they'd been happy once.

VIII

When she was fifty-two my mother fell downstairs on her head carrying my sister's daughter. The baby, who was two at the time, was unharmed, but my mother fractured her skull. The fracture healed and at first it seemed as if the only further damage was to my mother's nervous system. She lost her sense of smell and her sense of taste and, naturally enough, her skill and enthusiasm for cooking. But then, little by little, other things dropped away. She easily recognised her pre-war dancing partners on the TV, although I suppose in the case of Ronald Reagan she had opportunity enough ('Dull man, but frightfully good dancer'), but she started to forget her previous sentence halfway through the new one, and she would stare speculatively at her knife and fork as if unsure of their use. She started to cry in frustration when she forgot how to write the M in her Christian name, Minna, and when she took my daughter, aged four, to the village shop, a journey of a few hundred yards, my wife thought it safer to follow them as the two set off hand in hand, chatting simultaneously, uncertain who was leading whom.

For a while it seemed as if her behaviour was a painful plea for attention, and with the arrogance of self-interest I constructed a rational cause for her illness. I wanted it to be a psychological disorder rather than a corrosive physical decay of the brain. I wanted to believe that there was a reason for it: that she had been ignored and rejected by my father. I wanted her illness to serve my cause, but when I opened a door for her and she stared at the door, then at the doorway, and asked me with undisguised terror, 'Which side do I go?' I knew she was losing her mind, and that there was no one to blame except God.

Alzheimer's Disease is a terrible illness. If there is a physical disease it resembles it is leprosy, which eats away the body as Alzheimer's does the brain. The first signs are a loss of short-term memory, but forgetfulness, *non sequiturs*, and vagueness give way to loss of bodily control, as if the brain can no longer remember what to tell the body. The personality starts to disappear, and with it the humanity, and the soul, leaving, as if in mockery, only the body to breathe and be fed. The disease is spun out with a malicious cruelty, in my mother's case for ten years after it was diagnosed. Before that she was said to be suffering from 'Pre-senile Dementia'; it was the same thing by any name – she was old before her time.

For years she was losing her mind, and for years death seemed ashamed to approach her. Little by little she was slipping away, and we never knew when to say goodbye.

For a while she was living at home but it became impossible to look after her properly. She had bouts of terrifying rage, followed by incoherence, followed by blankness, followed by clear breaks of sanity that were more frightening to her than anything that had preceded them.

In most ways she had loved Dorset, and I have indelible memories of her, tanned and shoeless, dressed in a halter-necked cotton dress picking raspberries or tending the bull in the orchard on hot, carefree summer days, but her heartland was London, the world of her childhood, and when her mind became disordered she longed for that heartland as if her life, or her sanity, depended on it: 'Please, please, please, please, please, please . . . take me home . . . take me back to my mother . . . my friends . . . take me to London . . . let me go in a train . . . please, please, please, please . . .'

There was a silence, an absence of words and a despair so deep that it almost seemed as if her breath were speech, then a sigh: 'I think I am dying.'

But for years she lived on in the hospital, lying on the floor in a foetal position on a beanbag. No sight, no hearing, no sense at all. She breathed and ate and wasted away. She became an emblem for the nursing staff, and they treated her with great kindness and something like love. When the ward was turned into a surgical ward, and the patients decanted to private nursing homes in the name of 'cost-efficiency', they wept at her departure.

I would sit with her, with my hand on her forehead, year after year. She seemed inexpressibly lonely, but she'd seemed like that even before she lost her mind. Grief became muted over the years, but I never lost the distress of things unsaid. There are those who leave us without our detaining them; we have said all there is to say. It wasn't so with her; there was a continent of regret and guilt.

Her face and her body wasted away. Her mouth was set in the shape it became in the later years of her marriage when she was steeled in bitterness. I asked my father once when we were driving to the hospital, united for once in mutual despair, if things had been strained between the two of them for the last few years. Oh yes, he said, for about the last thirty.

I can still hear her voice even though it's hard to remember her face as it was before she lost her mind. I can still see her hand, bony like a claw, plucking at her face, as if she was surprised that it was still there. When I was a small boy I'd sit by her dressing-table to watch her as she did her make-up. 'I'm putting on my face,' she'd say.

When she died her body was like a child's.

It was a cruel paradox that my father knew he was going to die before my mother. He always seemed indestructible; when he became seventy he had lost nothing of his energy. He had acquired a girlfriend, and when my mother moved into hospital, his girlfriend moved in with him. For some time we regarded each other with mutual suspicion. Later I felt churlish in the face of their obvious happiness, but I found it difficult to forget my mother's distress in the early days of her illness when she suspected their affair, and suspected her sanity when it was denied.

My father's friend was a woman of about my age – large, loud, loving and tolerant (at least of him), and more often than not, like him, hiding her intelligence and sensitivity behind a wall of noisy banter. They lived like students, in an accumulated glacial deposit of old food, magazines, newspapers, photographs, sewing machines, clothes and crockery. They'd bicker and banter in his private argot which she had willingly learned even if it had become increasingly wearisome to those for whom it had been staled by overuse. They were content. 'Happy as pigs in shit,' my father would have said, and he must have been as surprised as anyone when he had a stroke. He'd gone up for a sleep in the afternoon, and at seven he hadn't come down. He was lying on the floor. 'I didn't know if he was drunk or something more serious,' said his girlfriend.

I went to see him and he could barely speak. Neither could I. Confronted by him – weak, vulnerable, mortal – I felt very shaken. He seemed terribly diminished, in terrible pain and worse depression, deprived of his energy and his mordancy.

A few days later he could speak. He told me that his mother had died of a stroke, his father had died of a stroke, and that these things are meant to shake you up; they are meant to change you.

He was moved to a new hospital and for a few weeks he occupied the same space in the same ward as my mother had seven years before. It was a deeply unsettling echo. I talked to my sister once on the phone after she'd seen him, and wrote as she spoke:

can't read
can't walk
won't try

He came home and his girlfriend looked after him with astonishing patience, enduring his rage and despair with unexpected equanimity. When he was seventy-four we gave a birthday party for him. He seemed barely to acknowledge me but at the end of dinner he made a speech, thanking everyone for their kindness, my sister and her children, myself and my family, his friends and his girlfriend. He staggered to his feet, and for a while – an eternity – he was unable to speak. When he spoke at last it was in short, uncompleted, bursts, choked with feeling like an overcharged light bulb, shining for a moment with great intensity, then breaking down in shuddering flickers. After a lifetime of guarding his feelings like Masonic secrets, emotion was breaking through in wild disorder.

A month or so later I had a letter from a vicar. He said he'd spoken to my father while he was in hosptial, and that my father had begun to make his peace with his Creator. My first reaction was pure incredulity. On the rare occasions that I had been in church with him, when he was in the Navy and, as Commander of a naval base, had to read the lesson, he had muttered throughout, noisily proclaiming his resistance to liturgy and his ignorance of the difference between a psalm and a hymn. Priests he referred to as 'God-botherers' or worse, and he'd always seemed to me defiantly resistant to the idea of life after death. Perhaps he was moved by the idea of retribution, or even forgiveness. Perhaps he was simply afraid of death. I don't think he'd bought the Christian line on suffering, but he did recognise one of the great moral equations, perhaps the only one: all our actions have their consequences.

The vicar was young and utterly guileless, and I think my father was touched by his honesty and lack of evangelical certainty. He asked me to help to put my father's 'house in order' before he 'faced the Evening Light'. The vicar recognised, he said, that he had not been an ideal father.

I went to make my peace with him. He was pleased to see me, coherent and shy of me. He knew, I think, what he wanted me to say and he knew that I was probably going to say it. We circled around each other for a bit, while the racing commentary babbled on the television; the Cheltenham Week. He asked me repeatedly when the Gold Cup was on. In two days' time, Dad, in two days' time. He said he hadn't fallen into dissolution yet, although some people thought he'd gone already, and, as if to prove that his memory was intact, he recited the name of all the destroyers in the Navy in 1938, eight different classes, followed by the names of his year at naval college – the Hawke Term at Dartmouth in 1929, thirty of them. He only stumbled on the last three.

His mind started to stray, and he said he had a terrible hangover. No, Dad, I said, you've had a terrible stroke. He said he'd been dancing all night; his ankles were swollen and he'd had to take to his bed. He'd woken up with three women and he'd had to prod them to make sure he wasn't dreaming.

'I'd like to be an oar,' he said.

'?'

'Yes, an oar.'

'What, like in a brothel?'

'No, idiot, *oar*.'

'Why?'

'It would be restful.'

He talked about the Fall of France; the day he got married. 'Send Ma some flowers,' he said.

'I'm bleeding, bleeding in my brain.'

I asked him about seeing the vicar. He was silent for a while before he said he'd got a great deal of comfort from him. 'One of the straightest men I've ever met. You'll find it a rich joke coming from me but I've been taking Holy Communion.' But I didn't see a joke, even though it was hard for him to speak to me without irony, or punning, putting his feelings in inverted commas, the habits of a lifetime. He struggled with the words, tears threatening. Until his stroke I'd never seen him cry.

'Was I as bad a father to you as my father was to me?'

'No, of course not. I wish we'd got on better, that's all.'

'He was a tyrant.'

'You weren't a tyrant, just a bit neglectful, perhaps. But I don't feel any anger against you. I love you.'

He gripped my hand, almost spasmodically.

'I don't know if I was neglectful, I just didn't appreciate you. I'm sorry if I made you unhappy. When is the Gold Cup on?'

'In two days' time, Dad. In two days' time.'

Then he paused. A long time. Minutes, perhaps, and, when my tears dropped on his hand, he gripped me tighter, and smiled, gently.

'Is Lucy a happy person? I hope so.'

She is happy, my daughter; it's a gift, like dancing.

He died in his sleep a few weeks later. Apparently everyone who dies in their sleep dies peacefully; I hope that's true. My sister rang me to tell me. 'Dad's gone,' she said. Just that. She sounded like him. And I said, 'Oh, he's gone.' Terse as ever with our feelings; we'd learned it from him. I was in a bar when Samuel Beckett died; it was on the TV. 'Ah well,' said an Irish voice. 'That's another one gone.'

I drove down to Dorset to see him before the undertakers took him away. The French writer Saint-Exupéry talks of 'seeing through the heart', and I've never seen the countryside around my home looking more intensely beautiful than on that day. Little churches, sandstone villages, valleys, hills, downland, slabs of incandescent colour – dark-green woods and hedges, fields of butter-yellow oilseed rape, blue of linseed, red of poppies, opiate-rich, and the barrows, lynchets, burial mounds, earthworks, ditches and standing stones of Celtic Britain. I drove up to Eggardon Hill, a few miles from our house. It's a Bronze Age hillfort that commands the surrounding countryside like an Aztec temple, an oval plateau dipping down hundreds of feet to woods and farmhouses and fields that stretch out to Golden Cap on one side, the sea beyond, and the Blackdown Hills of Somerset on the other side, and, with the exception of a spider's web of electricity pylons tracing across the valley, the landscape can't have changed for hundreds of years.

Sunlight hung over the hill like a benediction. I've always loved this place: it's vast and mysterious and awesome. When I was a teenager, rich in time and suffocating from boredom, I used to come up here and it felt like a foreign country. Now it seemed uniquely English.

I was brought up in a part of England that seems centuries away from the England I belong to now: the England of the city and the suburbs, of power and money, of art and politics, of poverty and people less lucky and privileged than I am, and I was. But this is where I started and something of who I am must be here, in this landscape, as much as in the body of my father.

He lay naked beneath a blanket, his arms crossed over his chest. He looked calm, at peace. He had shrugged off the tense, childlike, febrile look that he'd had for the past year. He looked very dignified and for once he seemed to me utterly authoritative and mature. My father. He had grown a beard, his last twitch of mild self-display, and he looked now like a patriarch, like Gielgud – all nose, and all English.

His skin was waxy and pale. I kissed his forehead and sat beside the bed. We end as we start. With the death of our parents we enter a second childhood, and once again confront the question: Am I loved? – but this time it's in the past tense. Only then, sitting by the dead body of my father, I realised what all my efforts had been for, why I'd been striving, what I was trying to prove. I'd been signalling, waving in a frantic semaphore: Look at me, look at me, look at me. Too late now. Whatever seam was available to me when I was very young, ways of making myself impressive to my father, I had exhausted long ago. When I failed I chose a life as remote from him as Antarctica. It was a means of advertising my independence from him, but I realised now it was another form of dependence – I'd been indentured for life. I had my freedom now; all I wanted was his love.

Mary Soames, who is Churchill's daughter, told me that she was sitting with her father in his old age late one evening. Long silence followed long silence. Then she asked him if there was anything in his life that he had wanted to do but hadn't, any honour that he'd wanted but hadn't received, anything that he regretted. And he said, 'I'd like my father to have lived long enough to have seen me do something good.'

IX

After his funeral we returned to the house, and I heard his voice. I darted into the room where he had died, convinced that I had heard him calling for me; a household ghost. I once saw a ghost in Cambodia. I went to Angkor, to the temples, when the jungle was a worse predator than Pol Pot. I arrived there from Hong Kong via Phnom Penh in a Royal Air Cambodia plane, one of whose two engines caught fire in flight. 'Excuse me,' I said to the stewardess, 'the wing is on fire.' The passengers, eleven of us, were consoled by a bottle of spirits apiece, and I travelled in more comfort to Angkor by bus, sandwiched on the front bench with the other privileged passengers – a handful of saffron-robed monks – while the remaining passengers, hundreds of them, clung to the inside, outside, and roof of the vehicle with children, chickens, pigs and vegetables carried like a second skin. All the way to Angkor, a day's journey, there was a constant cacophony of chatter, but what I most remember was the laughter. Within a few years all this had gone and the only laughter was the laughter of the grave.

When I arrived in Angkor it was getting dark, and after going to the hotel I walked to the main temple Angkor Wat. There was a full moon and I could see the vast scale of the temple quite clearly and the thick, serpent-shaped handrail over the bridge that crossed the huge moat to the main gateway. There are five, or maybe seven, I can't remember now, rectangular cloisters of

69

diminishing size surrounding a tower like a ziggurat in the centre. The outer rectangle is about a mile by a little less, and is lined by carved friezes, a bas-relief gallery that seemed to me to run for centuries.

As I passed through the outer wall I looked along an infinite colonnaded gallery. The bright white moonlight stabbed through the gaps between the columns and striped the floor like a giant animal skin; these patterns were followed by areas of shadow, whose black seemed so dense that they might have been solid. The wall carvings were in darkness, outside the edge of the slanting moonlight.

I walked for a while along the gallery and stopped in an area of shadow. Everything was still. Only the regular chanting of the crickets disturbed the pure silence of the night. I felt a small hand in mine, a child's. I looked down but I could see nothing. The hand led me towards the wall and placed my palm over some carvings – elephants, dancers, horses, warriors, Buddhas – I was guessing but it all felt like a seamless undulation, as if what it felt like was more important than what it was. When we reached a slab of moonlight I turned into the light, but the hand left mine and seemed to vanish. I could see nothing, and heard no breathing, no feet, no movement. The child, or spirit, had vanished as mysteriously as it had appeared. I've never known what to make of this encounter but I've never felt such tranquillity, such total lack of apprehension, as when my hand was pressed to the wall in that immense temple.

I told this to my father once. He probably wanted to show you his sister, he said.

I loved being in South-East Asia, travelling uncertain of my destination. I have always felt restless, a lack of a sense of place. I'm more at peace now, but too unsure to settle, as if to rest were to become dormant and to become dormant were a slow retreat to the fears of childhood. I have a love and a hatred of small villages; I long to belong, but I hate to be claimed. I have the same feeling about families: I envy what I imagine to be the enveloping security of a large family and the confidence that engenders, but I fear its inescapability at the same time. It's why I like the theatre, a surrogate family that has the advantage over the real thing of being temporary and of being chosen, rather than involuntary and for life and, oddly, if I like running a theatre it must be that something within me makes me want to play the father.

I don't think I had an unhappy childhood, even if I do sometimes still see happiness as the absence of unhappiness, like the relief of a dull ache. The body has a mechanism for forgetting pain; the brain is more stubbornly retentive.

We should never try to describe happiness. Like staring at the sun, you are blinded, you close your eyes, and there is an image left on the retina that is without definition. It fades and you are left with a blackness that is more bleak than before; an absence of light. We don't need to stare at the sun to see where we are going.

Sometimes I think of a time when I was happy; when possibilities hung in the air like motes of dust in the sunlight. I am driving with my mother, early in the morning, to Sherborne to take a scholarship exam at the school. It's a windless June day. We drive through woods, thick colonnades of tree shadows flick the black car as we pass. Through villages where the houses cast deep shadows on the road dark as reflections in glass. But for the car everything is motionless: cows, leaves, dogs, birds. My mother is wearing a wide-shouldered flower-print dress. I am wearing a school uniform, black blazer with maroon piping, grey shorts, and black shoes. My geometry set is sitting on my bare knees: compass, protractor, set-square, ruler. My mother smiles at me: 'It's going to be all right.'

I dream about this sometimes, and when I wake I want the journey to go on for ever.

ACTING PROPERLY

'Well, now that we *have* seen each other,' said the Unicorn, 'if
you'll believe in me, I'll believe in you. Is that a bargain?'
    – Lewis Carroll, *Alice Through the Looking Glass*

For a long time I wanted to be an actor. Like a stammerer I
wanted the gift of fluency, and like an orphan I wanted the gift of
love. The search for approval, for requited love, is the sustaining
force behind all actors; it's what sustains the bad ones and often
spoils the good ones. Insecurity is their fuel and I wasn't lacking
in that respect. What I lacked was the actor's Philosopher's Stone
– the talent that is more than a facility to observe your elders and
imitate them, more than a readiness to be the comic turn at parties,
more than a knack for dazzling the class when reading aloud, and
more than a dizzying simulation of self-confidence. If you don't
have it no amount of effort or education will compensate for the
injustice of having been cast out of paradise. Actors are born, not
made, but it took many years for me to accept that this truism
might also be true.

Like many children, I preferred to pretend to be someone else;
perhaps for no other reason than because it was so difficult to be
myself. I was part Walter Mitty and part Baron Munchausen,
and my tales from school painted me as the hero of my own
exploits, the star of my constellation, and, probably, the object
of my own affections. For much of the time I think I carried
it off, at least if the reactions of my mother and my sister were
anything to go by. But perhaps they were paying me the highest
compliment (but somehow the least welcome) that an actor can
receive: 'You didn't appear to be acting.'

My father was less sympathetic to my fictions. He had a

Churchillian phase during which, inspired more by the bricklaying than the oratory of his idol, he made paths and walls, once crushing his thumb under a concrete block and emitting a scream that was silent, as if he was searching for words to match the pain. He laid paths in thick, glutinous, grey, glistening concrete irresistible to a small boy. I walked barefoot in one of these when it was setting, and my father's rage was formidable even by his own immodest standards. 'It was Chico,' I said. Chico was a dog who looked like a soft-tufted lavatory brush and smelt worse but was, in all other respects, entirely innocent. The evidence of my footprint was indisputable but in my terror I imagined that the strength of my conviction in the lie, the force of my performance, would prevail. It didn't. I was soundly beaten, but not soundly enough to convince me that acting was outside the range of my accomplishments.

My performance as Peaseblossom in an open-air performance of *A Midsummer Night's Dream* at my primary school at the age of six did little to persuade me either way. I remember it only for Puck's habit of bursting into tears whenever she forgot her lines (frequently), and for making me aware of how difficult it is to sustain dramatic illusion against the intrusion of real life. During our scene with Bottom, who was equipped with a very notional ass's head, a horse, which had up till now been quietly and uninterestedly grazing in a field beyond our stage, contrived to open a gate, and strolled towards his fellow quadruped with a sort of speculatively seductive air. There was a great deal of screaming from the cast and the audience and a satisfying (at least to the cast) descent into chaos.

Like many aspiring (and aspired) actors I was shy, I was reserved, and I was more comfortable speaking in any voice but my own. The English get a lot of practice at this. Coded from birth by our accents, it's often more comfortable, or more liberating, to pretend to be what you are not. I acquired a skill as a mimic, partly as my passport, partly as a weapon. I was able to mimic my friends, our teachers, and for many years I was able to copy, like Chinese boxes, all the many voices of Peter Sellers – an actor, if ever there was one, who experienced a mortal difficulty in being himself. My enthusiasm for this vein of mimicry died in a restaurant in my early twenties. I'd just set out on the satirical travelogue: 'We enter Balham through the verdant grassland of Battersea Park . . .' and the words died on my lips as I caught the unamused gaze of Peter Sellers.

The only theatres in Dorset during my childhood were the Pavilion and the Alexandra in Weymouth, the Pier and the Winter Garden in Bournemouth. My mother occasionally took us to a pantomime there but I was as resistant as she was to the tyranny of audience participation, the witless slapstick, the graceless (and sexless) drag acts, the artless comic routines and the pretence that we were all enjoying ourselves. I hated the assumption that we'd all consented to this miserable ritual and, as supplicants, were expected to show our devotion in laughter and applause, but I liked the painted gauzes and the transformation scenes, and my heart always beat faster when the orchestra played the overture, the curtain rose and we were once again on The Village Green Outside the Baron's Castle. Many operas seem to begin in the same way and, as with so many operas, disappointment sets in rapidly.

I've seen one decent pantomime; it starred Stanley Baxter and Ronnie Corbett and was as different from the others as Nijinsky to Morris dancing. I find it sad that many people make their only visit to the theatre an annual penitential pilgrimage to the local pantomime, and it's little wonder that so few care to go inside a theatre again. Can there be anyone, apart from theatre antiquarians, who actally enjoys this pathetic annual parade of self-revealing national bathroom habits, fourth-rate comics, superannuated pop stars, has-been sportsmen, jokes about jokes about jokes about television, all of it marinated in the basest traditions of English 'variety'? Never was a word more inapt.

If variety is the spice of life (and it was in the case of Max Miller and Jimmy Wheeler) we saw precious little of it in Dorset. I did, however, see both Jewel and Warris and Morecambe and Wise in Weymouth, and although I am ashamed to say that at this distance I can't distinguish between them in my memory, I knew even then that I was watching something out of the ordinary.

My father didn't accompany us to the theatre but he would have enjoyed the pantomime that Roy Hudd told me about years later. At the start of his career Roy was apprentice and stooge to Jimmy Wheeler ('Ay ay, that's yer lot') who made no secret of his hatred of pantomime. He left the adult members of the audience mute and open-mouthed with horror, like the first-nighters in *The Producers*, when he invited the little boys to put their hand on the little girls' Polo mints, and the little girls to lick the little boys' lollipops.

Jimmy Wheeler was a comedian of the old school. It was Roy's melancholy task to wait behind for him after the show, standing outside the dressing-room while the comedian entertained a brace or so of chorus girls. After an hour or so of laughter, slaps, squeals, squeaks and the tinkle of bottle tops, the girls would spill out of the door, followed by an empty crate of beer, and the comedian himself: 'A very entertaining evening, Roy.'

This was possibly not far removed from my father's idea of an entertaining evening, but the nearest we got to it in the theatre was an annual visit to the Victoria Palace to see the Crazy Gang. They were the genetic link between music hall and the kind of comedy that started to appear on television in the late-sixties – Benny Hill with a hint of *Monty Python*. The sketches of the Crazy Gang were paragraphed by the routines of the Tiller Girls, 'sixteen long-legged lovelies', who linked arms, tapped and high-kicked like automata, wearing smiles that seemed printed indelibly on their faces. We sat, for reasons that were not then obvious to me, in the front row and I felt oppressed by the sheer bulk of buttock and breast and the acres of fleshy thigh encased in fishnet tights. I preferred the caperings of Flanagan and Allen, Nervo and Knox, Naughton and Gold, and 'Monsewer' Eddie Grey, who had energy and anarchy and the kind of seductive vulgarity that was the hallmark of Max Miller and the direct antithesis of the miserably bland TV comedy of the late-fifties – *Bilko* always excepted, of course. I can still see Jimmy Nervo, round, bald, pink and leery, being chased round the stage in a pram by Teddy Knox, chased by the rest of the gang as the audience rose to a pitch of fevered laughter.

I had a Pollock's Toy Theatre painstakingly cut with large, sharp scissors, scored and folded along the dotted lines, and stuck together with fishy-smelling glue. During the war, to while away the hours at sea when he wasn't on watch, my father had two hobbies: knitting and making small model steam locomotives from kits. The knitting produced a pink pig for my sister and a blue one for me, and the kits produced meticulously, and in my eyes miraculously, detailed miniature steam engines out of cardboard sheets the size of postcards. My father passed on the technique of model-making, but showed little interest in my toy theatre and less in the performances I staged with the two-dimensional cardboard cut-outs of characters from *The School for Scandal*. I think my apathy for the drama of that period stems from my frustration with the depressingly finite possibilities of staging a play with two hands and more than one character: I needed no less than three hands to slide the actors onstage while raising the front curtain or changing the backdrops. I should have bought cut-outs of Olivier and Jean Simmons in *Hamlet* – at least the scenery was simpler, and it's possible that I would have become a better actor with their inspiration, but somehow I doubt it.

I became bored with the limitations of my toy theatre and started to make puppets out of papier mâché – layered scraps of newspaper stuck together with flour and water, painted with poster paint and glazed with a thick, clear varnish. I liked the way that a puppet acquires its own personality: your hand becomes a metaphor for the body, the puppet a metaphor for the person. It's pure theatre.

A play with two characters is known as a 'two-hander' and

my hands performed duets that, like most improvised drama, were resolved in savage arguments and physical assaults, which cracked the lacquer on the puppets' faces and shredded the papier mâché like a pernicious skin disease. I deserted my puppets for Plasticene and, inspired by a lavishly illustrated location report in *Photoplay* of a Vincente Minnelli movie, made a model of a camera and film lights. The actors were recruited from my model medieval army – half a dozen knights in armour with lances and livery. They sat on horses, bright with their heraldic devices, and around them I deployed the camera, the lights, the flags, and the foot-soldiers from another century, and I still thought I wanted to become an actor.

The arc of my acting career describes a parabola shaped like an eighteenth-century military cap, or a bishop's mitre, bowing out at the side, rising to a peak (my university years?) and plunging, at first gently, and then with undignified haste, to the level at which I began. I didn't travel far, but at least I learned from the journey.

At my public school, initially at least, I was encouraged to act as I had been at prep school. Slightly against my will, and in the face of my instinctive contempt for its ennervating rhythms and wooden-topped melodies, I was cast as one of the Three Little Maids from a Sem-in-ar-y in *The Pirates of Penzance*. I was considered to have made a success of the part, but I was divided between being flattered and embarrassed at being told that I made a very pretty Kate. It was impossible to be unaware of the sexual potency of the situation: with our unbroken voices, our boyish figures, our unselfconscious flirtatiousness and an audience of teenage boys in a boarding school, not even the insistent blandness of Sullivan's music could extinguish the heat of androgynous sexual promise. No doubt the show was crude and maladroit, but there was enough there to alert me to the power of the theatre to excite and enchant – particularly with its sexual allure.

I don't think my experiments in cross-dressing in *The Pirates of Penzance* were enhanced by the large rugby socks that I stuck down my dress for breasts; my characterisation was all too literal, and my sexual identity had all the mystery of Violet-Elizabeth in *Just William*, but maybe, like all bad actors, I was simply trying to get the audience to look at me. If I didn't have the largest part in the play, at least, I thought with the prosaic sexual imagination of a thirteen-year-old, I could have the largest breasts.

Most female impersonation is satirical, underwritten by a palpable misogyny, but when it is done truthfully, observed with psychological and physical accuracy, it begs questions about the sexual roles we have been allocated. In a sense all acting, good or bad, is a criticism of life: human beings are represented and offered to us on a stage to observe and assess. In a wholly successful performance the gap between the actor and the character is seamless, and the judgements we make then are as confused, complex and ambiguous as those we make in life itself. But however well observed, in a performance that involves an impersonation of the opposite sex there will inevitably be a gap between actor and character; there will be an edge of comment, a touch of parody in the voice and the gestures. It will always be an imitation, never a state of being. Kabuki actors believe that women are too close to femininity to capture its essence; they mean its essence to men, of course.

Nevertheless, it's a marvel of the theatre that it is possible for an audience, regardless of sex, to look at a man playing a woman – even if his large feet and chest hair are visible – and believe in his femininity, just as an audience can willingly join the conspiracy to accept that a statue has come to life, or a puppet gained human characteristics. Like religion, the theatre can make us believe in the unbelievable.

There's a peculiar intensity to the way that an audience identifies with the actor and actress in drag: it is acting taken to its apotheosis, not only changing to another character, but another sex as well. Sitting there in the dark staring at an individual who is trying to impress you is a sort of sexual encounter, and if the sexual address is ambiguous, then that encounter is heightened. It's why the characteristic that all great theatre actors and actresses have in common is a touch of the androgynous.

Marlene Dietrich, who was a great star but far from being a great actress, used to say, 'I got into drag because I wanted to attract men and women.' Not me, I'm afraid. Her attraction for me was anaesthetised by her behaviour at the Lyceum Theatre in Edinburgh, where I was working when she did her *Late Night Show* at the Festival. Her conditions were stringent: the dressing-room must be decorated to her specifications, the Ballets Nègres from Senegal must be out of the theatre before she entered the stage door, and rose petals must be flown in from Israel in order to be dropped from the flies in a spontaneous gesture of generosity from the management after she had taken a score or two of curtain calls. When she came offstage after her first show, which I had watched from the wings, she was asked by a stagehand (he who had dropped petals on cue) for an autograph. 'Fuck off, darling,' she said. She changed quickly, went out of the stage door, stood on the bonnet of a car, and signed autographs for thirty minutes. When she died I heard on the radio that she'd visited her former husband after he had lost all his chickens in a landslide following a rainstorm in California. 'You should have stuck to ducks,' she said.

By the age of fifteen I had become a vicarious follower of the 'New Drama' – *Look Back in Anger, Roots, The Caretaker, The Hostage* and *The Long, the Short, and the Tall*. I hadn't seen any of these plays but I had read them and, at least as important, I had read Tynan's reviews of them. The attractions to a schoolboy of *The Long, the Short, and the Tall* were obvious: the story of a group of British soldiers and their Japanese prisoners in the Malayan jungle, it was bawdy (in so far – not very – as the Lord Chamberlain would permit), it was violent, it was funny, and it had an all-male cast. It couldn't have been long after its short run in the West End that we played it in the school hall to the satisfying disapproval of many of the staff and the undiscriminating praise of our contemporaries. I have a photograph of the production – against a serviceable set of a bamboo and corrugated iron hut and a primitive jungle backcloth, stand six or seven fifteen-year-old boys carrying rifles like large toys, their faces daubed with thick tan make-up (Leichner 5 and 9), painted beard stubble and glycerine sweat. We look like children engaged in a grotesque game, but, in spite of the make-up, not implausible. Most wars are fought by boys not much older than we were then. When I made *Tumbledown* I was told by a Falklands veteran that if the average age of the soldiers in the front line was much over twenty you'd never get anyone to fight. I didn't see any reason to doubt it.

I acted in two Shakespeare productions at school – as Benedick in *Much Ado* and Antony in *Julius Caesar*. I struck no sparks off my (male) Beatrice, but my Antony was alleged by a critic in the school magazine to presage a career as an orator. Perhaps if I'd played Macbeth my career prospects would have given more pause for thought. I was sufficiently swollen-headed by my notices for my housemaster, mindful of Antony's fate and my newly inflated ego, to tell me that actors were often taken over by the characters they played. With the exception of the inmates of long-running sitcoms, and the odd actor who, playing a character gifted with great sexual success, assumes that fiction can become reality, I've never seen this happen.

My performance as Antony had been crippled by seeing Brando in Joseph Mankiewicz's film of *Julius Caesar*. I idolised Brando and, as president of the Film Society, I was able to programme the film shows, operate the projector, and steal six frames of *On the Waterfront*, which I kept in my wallet along with two unused condoms for many years. I still regard Brando as the best film actor ever; he had – and maybe still has, but how would we know? – an almost mystical authority, great beauty, a persona that was mercurial, feline, melancholy, witty – and androgynous. He had the facility in spades that makes some film actors so alluring: the ability to appear to think slowly, so that the audience feels that it's being admitted to the intimacy of the thought processes, and embraced as conspirator in the emotions. Stage acting demands a radiant energy, a quickness of wit, a lightning ability to change thought and speech, and a virtuosity which, on screen, often makes theatre actors look like vulnerable show-offs. In the movies, they say, you keep everything in, in the theatre you let everything out.

Brando's unwillingness to work as an actor is profoundly sad and revealing. Something, I think, to do with the feeling that acting – 'play' – is not a proper activity for a grown-up, well, for a grown *man*. I have never known a woman to express this feeling. At a technical rehearsal, when the actors wear their costumes for the first time like anxious guests at a themed costume ball and stalk around the set like animals marking out their territory in a new habitat, it is inevitable that, at some point, at least one actor will say, 'Oh God, what a life for a grown-up.' Women don't share this problem. Maybe they are more used to being looked at, examined and assessed, or to having to pretend for the benefit of men, that a larger, paying, audience is a small shift of the imagination. Maybe they're more grown-up than men and consequently less anxious about their adulthood, or maybe they are simply unembarrassed by a process that is, after all, 'creative': giving birth – even if it is only to a character in a play.

After my expulsion from school, I became a barman and wine waiter in a restaurant in Somerset, and I continued to work there intermittently during my university years. I had qualifications enough – my 'work experience' from the age of eight as a waiter at my parents' parties. The restaurant where I worked had been started on the cusp of a social revolution; outside London it was rare then to find a restaurant that wasn't in a hotel, and as surprising as snow in the Sahara to find one that had cabaret and stayed open until one o'clock. They served modestly ambitious food and presented stars of the dying London cabaret circuit – Noel Harrison, who sang about the 'windmills of his mind'; Cy Grant, to whose Othello I was later to play Third Cypriot; Los Valdemosas, a Majorcan singing group to whom I lost my first four weeks' wages in a game of poker; and conjurors, charlatans, crooners, and undergraduate wits. The most memorable of the performers was a man whose name no one who is now under forty-five would recognise: Hutch. He was the authentic voice of post-war supper clubs like Quaglino's, Les Ambassadeurs, The Stork, names tinged with raffish, but faded, elegance. Hutch was black, romantic, effortlessly elegant: he sang with a touching grace and the ease and charm of Dooley Wilson in *Casablanca*. Hutch's song was 'This is a Lovely Way to Spend an Evening' and he sang it with an air of weary melancholy, which may have had something to do with having had to sing the same song for thirty or so years, but may have had as much to do with the way that women fell in love with him when he sang it. My girlfriend, who was French and a waitress in the restaurant, was no exception and he treated her with a practised courtesy and tenderness that I regarded with undisguised envy. 'Don't worry, young man,' he said, 'I won't be around much longer.' He died soon after and I missed him as much as she did.

Working in a restaurant was a rehearsal for working in the theatre, and I was attracted to it for many of the same reasons. As in the theatre you live to please, and of course, please to live. There's a satisfaction in being able to recognise your success as it occurs – the satisfied customer, the gratifying applause. If a restaurant manager is asking if everything is all right with your meal he needs your approval no less than the actor demanding the audience's applause. I found the hours attractive; I liked working during other people's leisure time, and having time off when everyone else was working. Being a night person gives you a sense of living by different rules, you can deride the tyranny of the daily routine. It's an illusion, of course – there's no more demanding routine than that of the actor in the long run – but it's a fantasy that sustains many actors, dressers, directors, and, I suspect, waiters and chefs.

I was the only English member of staff in the restaurant. There was the German manager, his Swedish wife, who worked as a waitress, a French waitress (my girlfriend), my fellow barman and wine

waiter – a surly, dough-faced Frenchman, and his irascible compat-
riot and room-mate, the chef – a tall man with a large Alsatian dog.
The dog bayed and barked with understandable anxiety whenever
the two Frenchmen made love to the Irish twins who worked in
the nearby hotel, while my girlfriend and I followed the catechism
of teenage romance: listening to Chopin, reading Verlaine, and
murmuring, 'Do you think it's right for us to sleep together?'

The day started at about eleven o'clock with clearing out the
empty bottles, and restocking from the store. The Irish twins
might wander in and mockingly tease me with accounts of their
sexual exploits that they knew had already been advertised for me
by the baying Alsatian. We'd have a few customers at lunchtime,
see a film or go to sleep in the afternoon, and assemble again
for the staff meal at six o'clock – usually the chef's best efforts
of the night. Then a long evening during which we worked for
five hours or so without stopping. We bantered like actors in the
wings whenever we passed on the restaurant floor, shouted at
each other backstage in the kitchen, winked, glared, and corpsed
above the heads of the unsuspecting customers who we regarded
with a kind of compassionate superiority, and who we served
with fixed smiles and courtly gestures as if we were engaged in
an exaggerated comedy of manners. When I was behind the bar,
I could listen to confidences exchanged, seductions made, partners
betrayed, friends defamed and retain an inscrutable deafness.

The last customers left about one o'clock and then we'd sit around
the bar dissecting the customers' characters and table manners, and
telling multilingual jokes while we played Twenty-one Aces with
liar dice – the first person to throw an ace chooses a drink from
the bar, the second pays for that drink, the third chooses another
drink, the fourth pays for that, the fifth drinks it. I don't recommend
the cocktail of malt whisky and Tia Maria but, as Groucho Marx
said, the great thing about whisky is that it makes you drunk.

I went to Cambridge in the early-sixties. It may not have been quite
then, as Larkin suggests, that sexual intercourse was invented, but

a few other practices were: pot smoking, academic vandalism, and undergraduate professionalism. I tried them all to a greater or lesser extent. I am no stranger to feelings of remorse, not least about my time spent at university. I was as wasteful of my time as a murderer's prayers.

I had taken my entrance exam in physics and chemistry and I knew, even as I sat the entrance exam, that this was not for me. I had learned my limits and for the first time in my life I'd discovered that it was impossible to bluff my way around my inadequacies. There are moments in your life when you confront the limits of your capabilities: you will never play the saxophone, become a polyglot, or ride in the Grand National. There are other things that you admit to never having the will to do: walking the Pennine Way, giving up alcohol for life, seeing the entire *Ring Cycle* or reading the novels of Barbara Pym. Perhaps these small defeats occur every day, but you adapt yourself unthinkingly to the known horizons of your personality. Beyond that there are genuine failures – expectations, or delusions, that have provided you with an identity that draws a thick, containing frame round your character. For me there have been two such sustaining fictions: 'I am an actor,' and 'I am a mathematician.' The latter died when I realised that, beyond the theorems and axioms that I could comfortably embrace, there were hypotheses and a language of speculative thinking that were as inaccessible to me as the mind of God.

I slipped into Cambridge on my science subjects and confessed my false pretences to the Senior Tutor who suggested that I changed to what he, enchantingly and temptingly, described as 'the humanities'. 'Try English,' he suggested, making a virtue of a necessity as the college had just invited Kingsley Amis to become an English supervisor and needed some students to justify their uncharacteristic act of free-thinking. Apart from nurturing one of the discoverers of the structure of DNA, and many solid but unexceptional right-wing clerics and histo- rians, the college's most celebrated feature was its well-endowed kitchens.

The influence, or at least the reputation, of Leavis was strong in the English faculty, and I always feel a little awed by those of my contemporaries who cite him as a potent influence in the formation of their literary thinking. Leavis is alleged (by Amis) to have sneered at my college for having appointed a 'pornographer', but, make of it what you will, I learned far more from Kingsley Amis than I did from F. R. Leavis.

I tried English, and I had a lot of catching up to do. My fellow students gave the impression of having been reading Pope while I was reading *Boy's Own*, but I made up for my prodigious ignorance by assiduously listening to jazz, reading the *Sporting Life*, researching the interiors of betting shops, going to the movies, and acting in as many student productions as would have me. I have made up for it since by becoming a voracious, even obsessional, reader.

University drama was centred on the ADC Theatre, which was housed in a converted cinema. It had most, if not all, of the technical apparatus of a modest repertory theatre, and in every sense tried to mimic the professional model to the point, I can see with hindsight, of extreme parody. Intrigues, jealousies, stars and careers were conceived on the lines of what were imagined to be the real thing. Actors vied strenuously for parts, and if rejected often started their own groups, shining in their separate constellations.

We were cocky, immodest, self-regarding, ostentatious, vain and self-important. Some of us may even have been talented. We were not especially iconoclastic; after all, the professional theatre of the day had at long last caught up with the cinema, and it seemed, and not only in retrospect, a golden age for the theatre. Barriers were broken in style, in content, in taste and in appetite but at Cambridge there were no eviscerations, no graphic sexual representations, and, apart from three semi-nude but wholly static Girtonians in a scene from *Expresso Bongo*, no nudity.

This was the occasion of my first, indelible, encounter with the press. Fleet Street had got wind of the intoxicating combination of female brain and body and descended *en masse* to seek names and photographs. The director of the show was Stephen Frears and he had his first taste of public controversy. I was its star and I got a no less edifying induction into journalistic blackmail. 'Are you intending to do this sort of thing professionally?' I was asked by a figure who uncannily prefigured the *Spitting Image* hack. I modestly asserted that I hoped so. 'Well, chum,' he said, like a baddie in a Basil Dearden movie, 'we can ruin you before you've even started.' He worked for a newspaper called the *Daily Mail*; I've read it with caution ever since.

A director is usually a cook; he assembles the best ingredients, follows his recipe and serves it up as impressively as he can. Occasionally, and very rarely, a director is an alchemist, transforming dross into theatrical, even real, gold. More often, however, a director is like a dowser or water diviner, trying to detect the potential that lies below the surface of an actor's talent. *Expresso Bongo* was a limp musical satire of the burgeoning pop industry, whose tunes gave ample evidence of why audiences were deserting the musical theatre in preference to the emergent pop culture. During rehearsals of this show Stephen sent me to a hypnotist. He was convinced that within my unpromising shell lay a rich seam of untapped talent, a Promethean vigour that could be unlocked by hypnosis. Alas, it failed; I was too anxious about disappointing the hypnotist, let alone the director, to abandon myself to the swinging watch chain. Even so I enjoyed a brief celebrity with my performance which may not have been entirely due to my proximity to the Girton nudes, but more to the gold lamé suit that I wore to sing several of the glutinously unappealing songs.

There were some of us who were involved in the theatre for the sheer pleasure of it, and there were as many who had their eyes on 'the profession', as it was awesomely described. There was a lot of talk about the preceding generation of directors (Peter Hall, John Barton, Peter Wood), actors (Ian McKellen, Derek Jacobi), and wits (Peter Cook and Jonathan Miller) as well as speculation as to who would be their successors. There was never much doubt about Trevor Nunn. I played Seyton in his first production of *Macbeth*, and learned from Trevor my first piece of theatrical jargon. Thinking that there was some urgency about muttering my first and only line, I raced on to the stage as if I were being chased by a swarm of wasps, fell to my knees and slid to a halt at the feet of the eponymous hero. 'TheQueenmylordisdead,' I gabbled. 'No, Richard, no,' said Trevor. 'Milk it.'

I'm ashamed to say that I remember the production most vividly for an incident of unforgivable irresponsibility in the ranks of the supernumeraries. For reasons not entirely clear to us at the time, eight monks crossed the stage diagonally at the beginning of the English scene. In the ranks of the monks we thought it would be amusing for one of our leading pair to put his monkish habit on back-to-front and we promised him that, given the difficulty of walking backwards in a straight line, he would be guided by a hand on his elbow. We set off across the stage; about halfway across his elbow was released, and, like a robot with a short-circuit, he careered towards an increasingly unnerved audience, who saw a lone, faceless monk with a mask of matted hair bearing down on them. Compassion overcame the remaining monks, and we sped downstage in perfect formation to retrieve our lost brother, who later became president of MENSA – which must say something about something.

At Cambridge there was a contagious condition that I didn't start to recognise until I had stopped being an actor myself and realised that I'd suffered from the same affliction. I've come to know it as 'university acting', although it persists in some actors long after their university years, and occasionally infects actors without a hint of higher education. It's the kind of acting that is all architecture and no heart, assembled by an intelligent mind conscious of meanings, of content, of style, of history, *over*conscious, in short, and saddled with an implicit editorial commentary that runs parallel to the performance, telling the audience what to think about the character and his predicament – and that the actor is more important, or more intelligent, than the character he is playing. It's like music written by computer.

Intellect, like beauty, is no bar to great acting, but beauty, unless it's animated by the breath of real talent, will seem gauche and plain, and intellect alone will make an actor seem doltish, describing a performance rather than giving it. I don't know a good actor who is not intelligent, but this intelligence is like a musician's, to do with timing, rhythm, hearing, sensibility, physical co-ordination rather than with cleverness and the ability to express ideas. Actors have more in common with spiritualist mediums than with dons, and the world of their work occupies a different globe to the articles of intellectual faith that underwrite university life.

I don't know that directors should be that much different. It has taken time in my case to learn to say, 'I don't know,' before rushing to rationalise, and I've learned to defend instinct against the intellect. It's not something I learned at Cambridge, which has been a breeding ground for a number of successful theatre directors. I have often heard it said that a kind of Mafia, or at the very least a Masonic brotherhood, exists in the theatrical profession among Cambridge graduates. While there may be a certain amount of circumstantial evidence for this, I don't believe it to be true. Opportunism has always been a more powerful bond than tribal loyalty. The privilege of Cambridge can't however be denied: there was a rare landscape of opportunity, well-endowed facilities, enough time, and a concentration of gifted actors. It was a sort of *de facto* directors' training course.

With the development of drama courses in several universities, the construction of university theatres, the expansion of the NUS Drama Festival, the elevation of the Edinburgh Fringe, and the voraciousness of TV and radio, student drama everywhere has acquired a much more conspicuous and egalitarian profile. Nevertheless, many of the newer directing talents, male and female, continue to emerge from Cambridge. Perhaps it's the water.

As for myself, I directed nothing at Cambridge but a short film that was plagiarised from Buster Keaton but which I've learned to describe as *hommage*, and I failed to prove to my satisfaction that I was a bad actor. That took a little longer.

I became a professional actor much as I might have become a soldier in the nineteenth century; I didn't seem to be fitted for anything else. Anyone can become an actor, all you have to do is to find someone to conspire in your delusion by offering you work – and obtain an Equity card. In my day you simply applied for one and paid a subscription, nowadays there's a little more to it; you have to serve a mandatory twenty-week apprenticeship. The catch, of course, is that to get the work you need the card, and to get the card you need the work . . . I heard the other day of an actress who'd been the stooge in a knife-throwing act to get her card; well, an actor always needs to be equipped to take personal criticism. I had no such training, and I embarked on my life as an actor armed only with my availability, my optimism and my defiant description of myself as a professional.

A friend of mine, a pianist, played the piano once for Bill Gore, a clog dancer who did a club act – dancing in coloured lederhosen. At the climax of the act the lights were switched off, and with the aid of ultra-violet light, the fluorescent clogs would come into their own. 'How do I see the music?' asked my friend. 'Use these,' said Bill, handing him spectacles with a torch taped to the side. 'Pro gig, lad.' My professionalism was much the same brand of wilful assertion: I advertised my services in *Spotlight*, the actors' catalogue, I went for auditions, I wrote begging letters to directors, I bought the *Stage*, I learned the jargon, and I railed about the injustice of 'the profession'. Eventually someone at Hornchurch Rep invited me to act for money.

My induction into the professional theatre was as inauspicious as is imaginable. After the long journey via Dagenham on the District Line, I entered a rehearsal room which had the air of a parish hall after an air raid. If people had been huddling under blankets it would have completed the picture, but in all other respects the image is exact; cups of tea, dour faces, inert bodies, an air of desolation and one energetic and voluble man who might have been the ARP Warden, but in this case was the director. He was attempting to engender sufficient enthusiasm in the cast to begin a read-through of the play, which was *Henry V*. The actors, most of whom had worked for him, looked about as likely to follow him once more unto the breach as into the doors of a gas oven.

'Hello,' trilled an actor I'd just met. 'Just joined the *Titanic*, then?' It's rare to encounter this degree of pessimism on the first day of rehearsal. More often the reverse is true – there's a contagious nervousness and self-doubt, but everyone is nevertheless determinedly optimistic. So much so that it often takes a wholesale evisceration of a production by the critics and mass defection of audiences to dent the optimism of a company of actors. It's usually possible on the first day of rehearsal to gauge whether the production is going to turn out all right, and at Hornchurch, even with my as yet untrained antennae, I could tell we were in for a bumpy ride.

Rehearsals proceeded from worse to terrible, and not even the replacement of the director in the third week (of a three-week rehearsal) could save us from certain catastrophe. Our spirits were kept alive by the remorseless camp banter of the wits in the company. Camp is the ghetto language of the theatre. It's not exclusively a gay slang, even if it annexes most of the characteristics of that argot; it's a way of looking at the world that seeks to deflect seriousness and asserts, at least on the surface, that nothing really matters. It's a different thing altogether from 'camp' in art, which is a critical term that describes high seriousness dressed up in implausible costume: post-modern architecture, Wagner's operas, Queen's videos, High Church liturgy. Camp speech is a levelling device (I heard it said of one of Hitler's speeches: 'Oh, she's in a right old state') and a lingua franca, like that of any closed society – the Army, rugby clubs, public schools, prisons or gentlemen's clubs. At heart camp is like the slang of nurses and doctors, a carapace against suffering – in the case of actors the suffering caused by failure and public humiliation.

ACTING PROPERLY

We were a collection of adults, some of whom were trained, experienced, and very gifted, and, like soldiers in the trenches, we were being sent out with no leadership and no protection between us and the audience but a few ill-designed costumes rented, or more likely borrowed, from someone else's conflict – a previous encounter with *Henry V*. I played Mountjoy the French Herald, in a costume that made me look like a rather worn playing-card. On my first entrance I faced a somewhat depleted but impish-looking English army. I spoke my first line: 'You know me by my habit,' only to be greeted by barely concealed gestures of self-abuse under the knitted chain mail. Later in the evening I doubled as a member of both the French and the English armies, who ran intermittently across the stage stopping only to fire arrows which bounced off the wall of the theatre and returned forlornly to the foot of the archer, who picked them up, ran offstage, changed a helmet, and returned in the other direction to repeat the process as the opposing army. I still smart with shame when I think of it and of the audience who endured it without criminally assaulting the actors and the management of the theatre.

Theatre is often embarrassing, inept, awkward, silly, in a word, tatty, and those who dislike the theatre cite its tattiness. One could say that it's as if you were to condemn Tolstoy for using the same medium as Barbara Cartland – but that's not really a serviceable analogy. While there's no danger of Tolstoy mutating to Barbara Cartland, there is *always* the danger of theatre, however fine, however 'grave', however 'serious', becoming absurd. At the moment of Lear's death, it only needs a member of the audience to sneeze loudly, or an actor to slip on stage, for the consent of the audience to be broken. However sophisticated its aims and its effects, it's never more than two boards and a passion, and it's precisely its ability to enchant, its *unreality*, that makes it so potent, but also, of course, so fragile. It's this very fragility of theatre, its potential for tattiness, that makes it so humane, so difficult and often, so absurd, and it's why one feels more comfortable sitting in theatres clad with 'humane' materials – wood, lath and plaster, faded gilt – than with unforgiving chrome and concrete.

No jobs followed, but at least none were lost, as a consequence of the Hornchurch débâcle. I was given a small speaking part (lost from the final cut) in a feature film, and I learned that the adage 'There's no such thing as a small part' is a pernicious lie. I felt as if I'd been taken out of a box marked *English Middle-class Male, Young*. I had no idea why I'd been chosen over the infinity of alternatives. At least when I went for an interview for a GUARDS cigarette commercial I knew why I was rejected. 'Too short,' they said as I walked into the room.

I had a part in a TV play. Rehearsals were conducted in a dilatory fashion in a church hall in Tooting. Actors were more raffish, or lazier, in those days, less concerned with 'image', 'career', and becoming 'personalities', and had yet to be soaked in the baptismal waters of the opportunism of the eighties and born again as pundits or politicians – which is really to say that there was more drinking at lunchtime and after an hour or so in the pub many of the cast were too tired to rehearse in the afternoons. So I'd walk round Tooting Market with Meier Tzelniker, who had once met Stanislavski and had worked in the Yiddish Theatre Company in Vilnius.

I was offered the opportunity of settling for a few months – a season at the Phoenix Theatre in Leicester: Play as Cast. The Phoenix is a theatre built cheaply, unpretentiously and wholly successfully in the early-sixties. It was next door to a bus depot, and lay parallel to a factory that made boiled sweets and glacier mints. I've not often recaptured the mixture of smells – acrid diesel fumes mingled with the vapour of sickly-sweet synthetic fruit and mint – but it's always recalled that period of my life with an almost nauseous intensity.

I lived in a bed-sitting room with peeling wallpaper, brown lino, a candlewick bedspread, gas meter, and a landlady who I only saw smile once – when I left. She was like the woman who a friend of mine overheard discussing a play she'd seen. 'How did you like it?' 'All right, if you like laughing.' It was not a glamorous life but, like most young actors, I was sustained in it by the fantasy that my life could be changed at the flick of a coin – stardom was just round the corner. If I'd been honest I would have had to say that my text was drawn from the film *42nd Street*:

> Miss Sawyer, you listen to me . . . and you listen hard. Two hundred people, two hundred jobs, two hundred thousand dollars, five weeks of grind and blood and sweat depend on you! . . . You've got to go on and you've got to give, and give, and give. They've got to like you, got to. You understand? . . . You're going out there a youngster, but you've got to come back a star.

This theatrical eve-of-Agincourt speech is actually as near as most accounts, fictional or documentary, get to describing what it's like to work in a theatre. Perhaps other professions are as ill served; journalists constantly complain of the poverty of fictional accounts of newspaper life – although I've never heard them trying to dispel the enduring and improbable stereotype of the Journalist as Hero. But like actors, journalists know that the reality is too prosaic and too dull to share with the public. To protect our fantasies we conspire in the fiction that life beyond the stage door is a combination of the Land of Oz, Dante's Inferno, and one of the more remorseless orgies of Caligula. I once met a brigadier who asked what I did for a living. 'I work in the theatre.' 'Mmmm,' he said, 'must be a lot of fucking.' To which I should have said, Not as much as either you, or I, would like, but probably no more than at the House of Commons, or *The Times* newspaper, or anywhere where there is a highly charged atmosphere, intense but carefully prescribed relationships, an air of sexuality, banter and fun, and hours that leave people of opposite, or even the same, sex together late at night.

Life on stage at Leicester was less fun than off, but at least I was learning. I was taught the meaning of 'blimping' from an actor who was playing Willie Mossop in *Hobson's Choice*; it meant being able to see up the women's skirts through the floorboards of his ill-constructed cellar. He later became a popular presenter on a children's show. I endured the wrath of an ageing actress in a sub-Chekhovian tragi-comedy; I was playing her servant – aged fourteen – and had to spend much of the play kneeling at her feet where she kicked me whenever she felt my concentration was straying. That wasn't unreasonable. It was more dispiriting to have to prompt Othello in his dying speech and then be taken by the neck as if *I* was the 'circumcis'd dog' when he killed himself, and that was not the worst of my indignities.

The production of *Othello* was a companion piece to *Henry V* and was watched by the audience with mute horror – as if they were watching a surgical operation performed without anaesthetic. It was acted in a style that I've come to know as 'dog acting', derived from the habit of actors in classical plays of seeking out a piece of furniture and placing a foot on it, uncannily resembling a dog's relationship with a lamppost. It's prevalent at all levels of the acting profession and is a sort of received idea of how to behave when encountering a classical text. It embraces sonorous voices, bombastic verse-speaking, and, because the language is heightened and archaic, a suspension of the normal criteria of human behaviour. Life stops being the model, and in its place a kind of coded conduct is substituted – pewter tankards clash, whores lift their tattered petticoats, lords laugh demonically, lovers coo and simper, kings bellow their authority, and victims are stabbed with the ease of a spoon entering a blancmange. It's very difficult to animate a text in a language that is alien to us – rhythmic, non-naturalistic, compressed and expressive, and it is rarely that actors are able to achieve it, particularly in the case of Shakespeare, without years of practice.

There are other orthodoxies of bad acting that can be observed in modern plays, and are endemic to most TV drama. How often have you seen an actor on TV finish a phone conversation and

stare at the mouthpiece, and how rarely have you seen anyone
do this in life? It is possible to see this sort of 'telephone acting'
spread, like echolalia, throughout an entire cast, just as in TV
sitcoms actors suffer from a collective deafness that necessitates
shouting at each other in ritualised exchanges which are resolved
only by bursts of synthetic laughter from a phantom audience.

We should be able to judge good and bad acting more easily
than any other art – after all, we are all practised observers of
human behaviour – but, given that, it's odd how audiences are
so easily contented with performances which, as Hamlet says,
'imitate humanity so abominably'. The truly real, or truly
natural, performance is rarely seen, and, perhaps, rarely desired.
An audience seems to want something more than imitation of
nature, something that is somehow different from itself. Often it's
fantasy that is required, but more often merely something that is
observably real and yet more exotic, more idiosyncratic, than we
feel ourselves to be. We want to be reminded of the singularity
of each human being, and at the very same time be made to
acknowledge that we swim in the common pool of humanity.

The Christmas show at the Phoenix Theatre was *The Boyfriend*.
There must be those in remote corners of the English-speaking
world who think that this pastiche of a pastiche of a twenties
musical is delightful, but I found its winsome melodies, its
saccharine charm, its camp, smug, self-regarding milieu, as
alien to me as an Aztec sacrifice, and at least as repulsive.
Like an advocate, the actor is supposed to remain detached from
the content – he is the servant of the play and not its judge – but
I was as impartial as a hawk with a dead mouse.

I wasn't alone; like prisoners of war counting flies, the chorus,
or at least the male half, developed their own survival techniques.
We sat motionless in our dressing-room before the show, our feet
on the table, staring inscrutably at ourselves and our colleagues
out of the corners of our eyes. The challenge was to see who
could be the last to get changed, made-up (regular Riviera tan,

Leichner 5 and 9), and get onstage for the first bar of the opening number. It was often the first note of the (shortish) overture that signalled an explosion of activity, with a degree of manic energy and commitment that disappeared as soon as we arrived onstage in our white shirts, trousers and deck shoes and told the audience that it was 'Nicer, much nicer in Nice'. Given our views on Leicester we could have sung that it was nicer in Anchorage, Alaska, with as much conviction.

My personal nemesis arrived when I came onstage, took my partner, and she whispered to me that she'd forgotten to put her knickers on. Mercifully the choreography was too demure to involve high kicks until the end of the number, at which point the girls dipped down on one leg, kicked high the other and leant backwards supported by their partner. A kind of laughter, like bubbles in a pan of thick soup, was building up inside me, and it burst as I dropped my partner on the stage in my efforts to defend her modesty. I stood still, shaking helplessly, until I was dragged offstage. Perhaps it was forgivable in the circumstances, but it was becoming clear, even to me, that it was unfair to release my contempt for my own inadequacies on a paying audience. I was beginning to think of acting as the Captain does of Joxer's singing in *Juno and the Paycock*: 'I hate to see fellas thryin' to do what they're not able to do.'

I decided to give up acting one Saturday afternoon just before the matinée. I can put a date to it: it was the 30th of January, 1965, the day of Churchill's funeral. I'd listened to the commentary in the morning, and on my way to the theatre I stood in a silent crowd outside a TV shop to watch the coffin conveyed from Tower Bridge to Waterloo Station along the river in a launch. Harold Wilson said at the time, 'There is a stillness and in that stillness each has his memories.' What my memories were I wasn't certain, and, although I felt profoundly moved by the funeral, I wasn't sure why. It seemed, and I don't think this is hindsight, as if a world had died with him. It was my parents' world, and in spite of my desire to see their world reformed, in my heart I felt only regret. Whether it was real or imagined, they were grieving for a lost utopia, an English Eden.

That afternoon I stared at my face in the mirror and felt like Magritte's portrait of a man looking at himself in the mirror; like him, I saw only the back of my head. I wasn't sure who I was, but at least I knew I wasn't an actor. I no longer had the will to continue. It was more than a lack of talent; I felt as if I'd been cushioned by a combination of exhibitionism and vanity, fuelled by sufficient confidence for the audience to supply the missing part and put it down to inexperience, and there had been enough co-conspirators in my fiction to encourage me to think I could earn a living out of acting. Confidence is nine-tenths of the business of acting, and when my cushion of confidence deflated I was left with nothing but despair.

I persuaded some of my fellow actors to be in a production of Ann Jellicoe's *The Knack*, which we performed on a Sunday night. After the performance, Clive Perry, who was Director of the theatre, said this to me, 'If you want to be a director, you can become one. I'm not sure you'll ever be an actor. But you must choose.' And I did.

Acting is a mystery: in the medieval sense it's a handicraft, and yet it's also something that is obscure, enigmatic, and beyond comprehension. All of us, consciously or not, are actors – we simulate feelings we don't feel, we lie, we pretend to be what we aren't. It is this latent, though well-rehearsed, skill that lures so many people to believe that they can become actors; if everyone does the actor's job in life, then anyone can do it on a stage. Couple this to a desire to assert an alter ego, and you go some of the way to explaining why the acting profession is so overcrowded with hopeful aspirants. It's a tantalising paradox that what seems so familiar and attainable to us should be so exasperatingly difficult to do; without talent, will, and character, it's impossible.

Good acting embraces a number of paradoxes: actors must be conscious of themselves, but not be self-conscious; they must know themselves, but they must also, on stage, forget themselves; they must be self-less, but will undeniably be selfish; and they must find the balance, while acting, between the heart and the head, reason and instinct, that Diderot describes as 'the true point':

> An actor who has only sense and judgement is cold; one who has only verve and sensibility is crazy. It is a peculiar combination of good sense and warmth which creates the sublime person; and on the stage as in life he who shows more than he feels makes one laugh instead of affecting one. Therefore never try to go beyond the feeling that you have; try to find the true point.

It's difficult to achieve this in life, which is probably why we give such extravagant praise to those who achieve it in art. To act properly, in life as in art, implies a moral dimension that makes us want actors to be exemplary beings. It's an impossible prescription – to seek attention for oneself but not to be narcissistic, to perform but not to show off, to communicate, but in someone else's voice – is it any wonder that actors often seem as ill-at-ease offstage as politicians outside the House of Commons.

The best actors have much in common. They know how to use a space and invariably make the space they occupy onstage or in the frame of a film seem expressive. The bad ones just stand there. Nureyev said, 'A great dancer is not one who makes a difficult step look easy, but one who makes an easy step look difficult.' It's the same with actors, the ability to transform the commonplace; to make gods of men, and men of gods. The best actors need to communicate with each other and with an audience; the bad ones never make contact, or make themselves heard. Courage is essential to the good actor; in the bad it is mere folly.

To express anything an actor must have a physical technique. It may be latent, but it must be trained. The training will always be empirical, learning by doing, and adding to that by watching other actors, listening to them, copying them, stealing their tricks, and reinventing them for yourself. Stanislavski was trying to give shape to an inchoate process; his 'Method' is a vast concordance of common sense. The fact that few, if any, good actors invoke his work is not to say that they don't recognise and follow most of his pragmatic precepts.

I'm never surprised that the question that actors are most often asked is not, 'Who are you sleeping with?' but, 'How do you learn your lines?' The question is not naive; what should be inferred from it is the desire to know how another human being transforms themselves into another. It is a form of magic, as mysterious as the ability to conjure sweet sounds out of a piece of varnished wood with catgut stretched over it.

There are as many 'methods' of working as there are actors, and, unless they are subject to the collective discipline of an expressionistic production or of a musical, most actors will work like scavengers, picking up ideas, images, 'business', and occasionally, like panhandlers, pure gold. A structure is imposed on an actor's work by the rehearsal process; the lines acquire meaning, the moves evolve, ideas become animated, against a rigid and remorseless storyline – rehearsals begin at a known point, they end some weeks later when the play is decanted (sometimes disastrously) from the rehearsal room to the stage. There is always a result: a triumph, or a catastrophe – or, more often, something in between. During the rehearsal period some gifted actors seem exasperatingly slow, some bewilderingly stubborn, some alarmingly quick, leaping from conclusion to conclusion like scaffolders on rooftops.

For all the disparate ways of working, and the apparent self-absorption and navel-watching, there is one inviolable rule: you have to play with your fellow actors – the solipsist will always be left marooned on an island of his own making. Strong actors can appear, often unfairly, to dominate a rehearsal and a stage at the expense of other actors. They radiate an energy that has an almost physical heat, and, like poultices, they draw the heat from the actors who surround them. Being combative, impatient, irascible, and frustrating is often an implicit demand to be challenged and stimulated, to be given competition by their fellow actors. Even accounting for this, some actors seem to need to make it difficult for themselves, even painful. It's as if they are fighting to achieve a mystical dimension by suffering, when that dimension, which unquestionably exists, is achieved only by practical means.

Take any actors, and you will find their working methods are as distinct as their personalities and backgrounds. To take three actors, not entirely at random: Judi Dench, Ian McKellen, and Michael Bryant. None of them would confess to a working 'method', any more than they would own up to a 'lifestyle', but they all have processes that they have, consciously or not, developed over many years; serendipity may play a part in their work, but little that they do is accidental. Judi Dench is an actress who works almost entirely on her instincts. Someone once told me that John Williams, the guitarist, never needed to practise, his technique is effortless. Like him Judi has technique to burn – she can turn a line on a fragment of a syllable, a scene on the twist of a finger. She doesn't *study* a part but works through a process of osmosis, soaking up the details with a sometimes disconcerting randomness. She'll ask questions that seem hardly to bear on the character and, as if she'd disturbed you while reading a book, leave you as soon as you answer as if afraid that more talking would muddy the instinct. When I directed her in *The Cherry Orchard* for TV, she beckoned to me thoughtfully just before we went for a take; it was a long scene in which Ranyevskya talks about her life with her lover in France. 'She's a terrible old tart, isn't she?' she said, with a mixture of charity and envy. When she's rehearsing the elements of her performance seem disparate but gradually, and invisibly, the elements come together: head, heart, voice and body into a marvellous synchronicity. She reminds me of what Peggy Ramsay told me once about recognising whether an actor is in character, 'Look at the feet, dear.'

At first glance Ian McKellen is a scientific actor. His performances form like crystals in a saturated solution; you hang a small crystal from a thread and little by little, facet by facet, the crystal grows until it hangs like a large diamond. As a young actor he wore his talent like a jewel, turning it in the light, holding it up for the audience to marvel at, but over the years, as his public and private life have fused, so have his talent and his character. It's not always true of actors, and of people in general, that they desire to improve themselves; in this sense Ian is exemplary. 'Everyone has talent at twenty-five,' said Degas. 'The difficulty is to have it at fifty.'

Some actors start with trying to establish the details of how the character will look, some with how they will think or feel. It was said of Olivier that he started with the shoes; with Ian it's the face and the voice. I have a postcard he sent me when we started to work on *Richard III* – a wry cartoon of a severe face, recognisable as his own, with sharply receding hair, an arrow pointing to a patch of alopecia; at the throat is a military collar, above the shoulder the tip of a small hump. He is a systematic, fastidious and exacting actor; each word is picked up and examined for its possible meanings, which are weighed, assessed, discarded or incorporated. In rehearsals he is infinitely self-aware, often cripplingly so. His waking, and perhaps sleeping, dreams are of how he will appear on stage – his position, his spatial relationships with the other actors. But in performance that inhibition drops away like a cripple's crutches and he is pure performer. All the detail that has been so exhaustively documented becomes a part of an animate whole. In sport, in a great performance, there must always be an element of danger. The same is true of the theatre. I wouldn't say there is not a good or even effective actor without this characteristic, but there is certainly no celebrated one.

After acting with Ian, Irene Worth said, 'We were jazzing.' Like a musician, he composes his performances; he writes a score for his own orchestral forces and then allows himself to conduct it. Sometimes you can see the conductor at work, but more often the conductor becomes subsumed in the character and what you are watching is an act of possession.

The most mysterious, even mystical, element in acting is the element that has the characteristics of demoniacal possession – the phenomenon in which the devil besets the soul inside the body, when Satan is said to 'inhabit' the victim. Virtuous people were supposed to be immune from it, and perhaps the facility of actors to be possessed not by demons but by the characters they are playing has made some contribution to the fiction that they are in some way less virtuous than the normal run of society.

The phenomenon of possession is often apparent in flashes during rehearsals when an actor suddenly develops a particular rhythm, an inner ear for the character, and the voice and movements of his body no longer seem his own. It is as if, rather than the actor occupying the character, the character has occupied the actor. During an early run-through of a play, the actors are always charged with a febrile nervous energy, and at this point the 'spirit' of the character often seems to drive the actor's imagination and invention, and things that have never happened in rehearsals occur spontaneously and effortlessly. It is almost unnerving to see the actor's own personality, which may be quiet, unforceful, and inarticulate, be wrenched, thrown about, transformed, and, literally, possessed by another persona. At the end of the run-through, when this has occurred, the actor is left exhausted, etiolated, as if the 'spirit' has departed and left him to learn how to summon the demon again, and how to harbour and accommodate it. In effect, the actor's problem is how to repeat the experience without the wasteful energy; an actor cannot live the experience every time, he must learn to simulate it. This is the true test of the professional – he or she must experience possession, endure passion and yet, like a firewalker, remain untouched by the experience.

For all its sensational associations, it's a remarkably unsensational event to witness. To some degree it's an essential part of all rehearsals and, if not entirely taken for granted by actors, is no more celebrated than the rising of a soufflé would be by a chef. Audiences take it for granted and recognise the phenomenon only when it's inescapable – in Edna Everage, for instance, when they're struck over the head with a gladiolus by a rather studious, thoughtful, mild-mannered man.

There are those, and not only from primitive societies, who hate to be photographed; they feel that it steals their soul. Paradoxically, some actors, when they are unprepared, out of character or rehearsing, feel the same, and they conceal themselves behind a prickly wall. Maggie Smith is one of these. Onstage she is luminous, brilliant and wholly accessible to the public, and in private, she is – well, private. I made a film with her of a Tennessee Williams play. For much of the time she was not feeling well, and was enduring conditions that would have tested my namesake along the Great Australian Bight: shooting over eight minutes of dialogue a day in a studio with the temperature rising to 110°F, and the humidity of a tropical rain forest. Maggie said that she felt like Alec Guinness in *The Bridge on the River Kwai*; I felt more like the Camp Commandant. And yet, when I look at her now on the screen, there is an effortlessness in her performance that shows nothing of the pain. It is not merely that she acts with astonishing skill, she seems to render the description of 'acting' inapplicable; alchemy would be more appropriate. Her playing of the half-mad Mrs Venable doesn't seem like imitation; it seems more like theft – she has stolen her soul.

Most actors hate to talk about their work; they are rightly reluctant to intellectualise about processes that are idiosyncratic and instinctive. Alfred Molina, a hugely gifted, droll, mercurial actor, insists that acting is just a matter of mechanics, and yet when you work with him you witness an invention, and intensity of intuition and feeling that is anything but mechanical. Miranda Richardson appears to have a translucently thin skin as an actress; you can almost *see* the feelings. She has an unearthly ability to transform herself, but you will discover no more about how she does it than you will about the plant life on Mars. Robert Stephens said in an interview, 'I have no great views about acting except this. Number one: If you are going to act be serious about it. Number two: For God's sake speak properly.'

Michael Bryant is firmly of this persuasion. To hear him talk you would imagine he is a carpenter or a farmer, and is as reluctant to theorise about acting as about a piece of wood or a cow. He has as much interest in 'experiment' and 'research' as a farmer has in veterinary science or a carpenter in tree surgery. When he was rehearsing *Wind in the Willows* Nicholas Hytner invited the actors to study the behaviour of their respective animals: toads, rats, weasels, ferrets, rabbits and badgers. Michael took a video of a badger-watch away with him and returned a day or two later with this revelation: 'I have made a discovery about the habits of badgers: their movement and their posture has an extraordinary resemblance to Michael Bryant.'

Actually, in his approach to a part he reminds me most of a badger-watcher: silent, strategic, patient, unobtrusive; he stalks a part. He talks little in rehearsal and needs, or wants, only the most basic information – where he is to stand, what the furniture is, louder, softer, quicker, slower. He regards the text as the only hard evidence at his disposal, and matter-of-factly builds his character like a detective assembling a case until one day, sometimes alarmingly late in rehearsal, the character is there – complete. It's if he'd been marinating the part in secret until it was ready, and if you enquired about the recipe you would be bluntly rebuffed. Yet for all his blimpish, witty, portly, plain-man persona, there is no actor more sensitive, more subtle, or more private than Michael Bryant. If the mystery of acting is the combination of craft and enigma, no one embodies it more fully – to which I can hear him saying, 'Oh bollocks!'

'Scratch an actor,' said Laurence Olivier, 'and you find an actor.' He should have known, but I don't think it's true, or any more true of actors than politicians, or priests, or teachers, or strippers, or anyone else engaged in acts of public self-display. What *is* true, I think, is that if you scratch an actor you will find a child. Not that actors are inherently less mature than politicians, priests, etc, but actors must retain a child's appetite for mimicry, for demanding attention, and above all for playing. They must see with a child's heart, innocent of judgement.

Like all children (and all artists), actors crave approval. With actors the craving is more acute than in other performers, because you cannot make the distinction between approving the performance and approving the actor himself. In applauding the performance, like a grateful parent, you are bestowing love not on a fiction but on the actor who stands before you.

Directors are far from immune from the desire for approval, even if they are more insulated than actors from the raw immediacy of rejection. When I first became a director I visited the Odeon Theatre in Paris; it is still my favourite theatre in the world, inside and out. I saw Jean-Louis Barrault play there, and imagined, as I watched, that a production of mine might one day occupy that stage. In 1990 I took *Richard III* there, and at the end, in the amiable tradition of European theatre, I was pushed onstage to take my bow with the actors. I walked forward like a sleep-walker, gazing at the audience as if surprised that it had intruded on my dream. 'Bow,' hissed Ian McKellen. 'You BOW.' I did, and felt the intense pleasure of what for an actor is all in a night's work; love requited.

PEOPLE

GRANVILLE-BARKER

The history of the theatre in England in this century can be told largely through the lives and work of two men: George Bernard Shaw and Harley Granville-Barker, a triple-barrelled cadence of names that resonates like the ruffling of the pages of a large book in a silent public library. One was a brilliant polemicist who dealt with certainties and assertions and sometimes, but not often enough, breathed life into his sermons; the other a committed sceptic who started from the premise that the only thing certain about human behaviour was that nothing was certain. Both, however, possessed a passionate certainty about the importance of the theatre and the need to revise its form, its content, and the way that it was managed. Shaw was a playwright, critic and pamphleteer, Barker a playwright, director and actor.

The Voysey Inheritance is, at least in my opinion, Granville-Barker's best play: a complex web of family relationships, a fervent, but never unambiguous, indictment of a world dominated by the mutually dependent obsessions of greed, class, and self-deception. It's also a virtuoso display of stagecraft: the writer showing that as director he can handle twelve speaking-characters on stage at one time, and that as actor he can deal with the most ambitious and unexpected modulations of thought and feeling. The 'inheritance' of the Voyseys is a legacy of debt, bad faith, and bitter family dissension. Edward's father has, shortly before his death, revealed that he has been cheating the family firm of solicitors for many years, as his father had for many years before that. Towards the end of the play Edward Voysey, the youngest son, confronts the woman he loves:

EDWARD: Why wouldn't he own the truth to me about himself?

BEATRICE: Perhaps he took care not to know it. Would you have understood?

EDWARD: Perhaps not. But I loved him.

BEATRICE: That would silence a bench of judges.

Shaw would have used the story to moralise and polemicise. He might have had the son hate the father; he might have had him forgive him; he might have had him indict him as a paradigm of capitalism; he would never have said he loved him.

Everybody needs a father, or, failing that, a father figure. He may be a teacher, a prophet, a boss, a priest, perhaps a political leader, or a friend. If you can't find a father you must invent him. In some ways, not altogether trivial, Granville-Barker is something of a father figure for me. He's a writer who I admire more than any twentieth-century English writer before the sixties – Chekhov with an English accent; he's the first modern British director; he's the real founder of the National Theatre, and, in his *Prefaces*, he's a man who, alone amongst Shakespearian commentators before Jan Kott, believed in the power of Shakespeare on stage.

There was a myth that Granville-Barker was the natural son of Shaw. He was certainly someone who Shaw could, in his awkward way, cherish and admire, educate and castigate. When Barker fell wildly in love ('in the Italian manner' as Shaw said) with Helen Huntington, an American millionairess, he married her, acquired a hyphen in his surname, moved first to Devon to play the part of a country squire, and then to France to a life of seclusion. Shaw thought that he had buried himself alive and could never reconcile himself to the loss. It was, as his biographer Hesketh Pearson said, 'The only important matter about which he asked me to be reticent.'

After directing many of Shaw's plays for many years, acting many of his best roles (created with him in mind), dreaming and planning together the birth of a National Theatre, not to mention writing, directing, and acting in his own plays while managing his own company at the Royal Court, Barker withdrew from the theatre, and for twenty years there was silence between the two men. Only on the occasion of the death of Shaw's wife did they communicate by letter. 'I did not know I could be so moved by anything,' wrote Shaw to him.

Out of this self-exile came one major work, slowly assembled over many years: *The Prefaces to Shakespeare*. With a few exceptions (Auden on *Othello*, Barbara Everett on *Hamlet*, Jan Kott on *The Tempest*) it's the only critical work about Shakespeare that's made any impact on me, apart, that is, from my father whose view of Shakespeare was brief and brutal: 'It's absolute balls.'

As much as we need a good father, we need a good teacher. Mine, improbably perhaps, was Kingsley Amis. He'd arrived, somewhat diffidently, at Cambridge at the same time as I did. The depth of my ignorance of English literature corresponded almost exactly to his dislike of the theatre. Nevertheless, he made me see Shakespeare with a mind uncontaminated by the views of academics, who he would never have described as his fellows and whose views he regarded as, well, academic. I would write essays marinated in the opinions of Spurgeon, Wilson Knight, Dover Wilson and a large cast of critical supernumeraries. He would gently, but courteously, cast aside my essay about, say, *Twelfth Night*: 'But what do you think of this play? Do you think it's any good?' 'Well . . . er . . . it's Shakespeare.' 'Yes, but is it any *good*? I mean as a *play*. It says it's a comedy. Fine. But does it have any decent jokes?'

I took this for irreverence, heresy even. Over the years, however, I've come to regard this as good teaching, or, closely allied, good direction. It's asking the right questions, unintimidated by reputation, by tradition, by received opinion, or by critical orthodoxy. This was shocking, but healthy, for a young and impressionable man ripe to become a fundamentalist in matters of literary taste and ready to revere F. R. Leavis as the Ayatollah of 'Cambridge English'. What you have is yourself and the text, only that. That's the lesson of Granville-Barker: 'We have the text to guide us, half a dozen stage directions, and that is all. I abide by the text and the demands of the text and beyond that I claim freedom.' I can't imagine a more useful and more enduring dictum.

The Prefaces have a practical aim: 'I want to see Shakespeare made fully effective on the English stage. That is the best sort of help I can lend.' What Granville-Barker wrote is a primer for directors and actors working on the plays of Shakespeare. There is lamentably little useful literature about the making of theatre, even though there is an indigestible glut of memoirs and biographies, largely concerned with events that have taken place *after* the curtain has fallen. If I was asked by a visiting Martian to recommend books that would help him, her or it to make theatre in the manner of the European I could only offer four books: Stanislavski's *The Art of the Stage*, John Willet's *Brecht on Brecht*, Peter Brook's *The Empty Space*, and *The Prefaces to Shakespeare*.

Stanislavski offers a pseudo-scientific dissection of the art of acting which is, in some respects, like reading Freud on the mechanism of the joke: earnest, well-meaning, but devoid of the indispensable ingredient of its subject-matter: humour. Stanislavski's great contribution was to demand that actors hold the mirror up to nature, that they take their craft as seriously as the writers who they served, and to provide some sort of formal discipline within which both aims could be realised.

Brecht provided a manifesto that was a political and aesthetic response to the baroque encrustations of the scenery-laden, star-dominated, archaic boulevard theatre of Germany in the twenties. Although much of what he wrote as theory is an unpalatable mix of political ideology and artistic instruction, it is his theatrical instinct that prevails. He asserts, he insists, he browbeats. He demands that the stage, like society, must be reexamined, reformed, that the audience's habits mustn't be satisfied, they must be changed, but just when he is about to nail his Thirteen Articles to the church door he drops the voice of the zealot: 'The stage is not a hothouse or a zoological museum full of stuffed animals. It must be peopled with live, three-dimensional, self-contradictory people with their passions, unconsidered utterances and actions.' In all art forms, he says, the guardians of orthodoxy will assert that there are eternal and immutable laws that you ignore at your peril, but in the theatre there is only one inflexible rule: 'The proof of the pudding is in the eating.' Brecht teaches us to ask the question: What goes on in a theatre?

Brook takes that question even further: What is theatre? It's a philosophical, but eminently practical, question that Brook has been asking for over thirty years and which has taken him to the African desert, a quarry in Iran, and an abandoned music hall in Paris. 'I take an empty space and call it a bare stage. A man walks across this empty space while someone else is watching him, and that is all that is needed for an act of theatre to be engaged.' For all his apparent concern with metaphysics, there is no more practical man of the theatre than Brook. I was once at a seminar where someone asked him what was the job of the director. 'To get the actors on and off stage,' he said. Like Brecht, like Stanislavski, like Granville-Barker, Brook argues that for the theatre to be expressive it must be, above all, simple and unaffected: a distillation of language, of gesture, of action, of design, where meaning is the essence. The meaning must be felt as much as understood. 'They don't have to understand with their ears,' says Granville-Barker, 'just with their guts.'

Brecht did not acknowledge a debt to Granville-Barker. Perhaps he was not aware of one, but it seems to me that Barker's Shakespeare productions were the direct antecedents of his work. He certainly knew enough about English theatre to know that he was on to a good thing adapting *The Beggar's Opera, The Recruiting Officer* and *Coriolanus*. Brecht has been lauded for destroying illusionism; Granville-Barker has been unhymned. He aimed at reestablishing the relationship between actor and audience that had existed in Shakespeare's theatre – and this at a time when the prevailing style of Shakespearian production involved *not* stopping short of having live sheep in *As You Like It*. He abolished footlights and the proscenium arch, building out an apron over the orchestra pit which Shaw said 'Apparently trebled the spaciousness of the stage . . . To the imagination it looked as if he had invented a new heaven and a new earth.'

His response to staging Shakespeare was not to look for a synthetic Elizabethanism. 'We shall not save our souls by being Elizabethan.' To recreate The Globe would, he knew, be aesthetic anaesthesia, involving the audience in an insincere conspiracy to pretend that it was willing collaborator in a vain effort to turn the clock back. His answers to staging Shakespeare were similar to Brecht's for *his* plays and, in some senses, to Chekhov's for his. He wanted scenery not to decorate and be literal, but to be expressive and metaphorical, and at the same time, in apparent contradiction, to be specific and real, while being minimal and iconographic: the cart in *Mother Courage*, the nursery in *The Cherry Orchard*, the dining table in *The Voysey Inheritance*. 'To create a new hieroglyphic language of scenery. That, in a phrase, is the problem. If the designer finds himself competing with the actors, the sole interpreters Shakespeare has licensed, then it is he that is the intruder and must retire.'

In *The Prefaces* Granville-Barker argues for a fluency of staging unbroken by scene changes. Likewise the verse should be spoken fast. 'Character in action, not sound like the voice beautiful from the lectern . . .' 'Be swift, be swift, be not poetical,' he wrote on the dressing-room mirror of Cathleen Nesbitt when she played Perdita. Within the speed, however, detailed reality: *meaning* above all.

It is the director's task, with the actors, to illuminate the meanings of a play; its vocabulary, its syntax, and its philosophy. The director has to ask what each scene is revealing about the characters and their actions: what story is each scene telling us? In *The Prefaces* Granville-Barker exhumes, examines and explains the lost stagecraft of Shakespeare line by line, scene by scene, play by play.

Directing Shakespeare is a matter of understanding the meaning of a scene and staging it in the light of that knowledge. Easier said than done, but it's at the heart of the business of directing any play, and directing Shakespeare is merely directing writ large. Beyond that, as David Mamet has observed, 'choice of actions and adverbs constitute the craft of directing'. Get up from that chair and walk across the room. Slowly.

With Shakespeare as with any other playwright the director's job is to make the play live, now, in the present tense. 'Spontaneous enjoyment is the life of the theatre,' says Granville-Barker in his Preface to *Love's Labour's Lost*. To receive a review, as Granville-Barker did, headed SHAKESPEARE ALIVE! is the most, but should be the least, that a director must hope for.

I regard Granville-Barker not only as the first modern English director but as the most influential. Curiously, partly as a result of his early withdrawal from the theatre, partly because his *Prefaces* have been out of print for many years, and partly because of his own self-effacement, he has been unjustly ignored both in the theatre and in the academic world, where the codification of their 'systems' has resulted in the canonisation of Brecht and Stanislavski.

My sense of filial identification is not entirely a professional one. When I directed *The Voysey Inheritance* I wanted a photograph of the author on the poster. A number of people protested that it was the height, or depth, of vanity and self-aggrandisement to put my own photograph on the poster. I was astonished, I was bewildered, but I was not unflattered. I still can't see the resemblance and it's not through lack of trying.

Two years ago the Royal National Theatre was presented with a wonderful bronze bust of Granville-Barker by Katherine Scott (the wife, incidentally, of the Antarctic hero). For a while it sat on the windowsill of my office like a benign household god. Then it was installed on a bracket in the foyer opposite a bust of Olivier, the two men eyeing each other in wary mutual regard. A few months later it was stolen; an act of homage, perhaps. I miss him.

OLIVIER

The last time Olivier came to the National was on the occasion of his eightieth birthday. A gala evening had been arranged, one of those elephantine occasions that stand in danger of being suffocated under a blanket of earnest and well-meant litanies of adulation. I'd only just been made Director Designate of the National Theatre, and so I was standing rather diffidently by the stage door waiting for Olivier in the ample shadow of Peter Hall. There was an enormous crowd and hordes of paparazzi in the street. The atmosphere was somewhere between St Peter's Square before the appearance of the Pope on the balcony, and the entrance to one of the large hotels before an awards ceremony to which Joan Collins has been invited.

As the car pulled up there was a wail from the crowd, almost Iranian in its tone and intensity, and out of the car stepped Olivier, smaller, almost unrecognisably so, a very, very frail man supported by Joan Plowright. There was a cascade of flash bulbs and screams and hoots. For a moment he was completely dazed. Then he moved slightly towards the crowd, hesitating between terror and intense joy.

At the same moment Peter Hall started to move to welcome him, his arms outstretched in greeting. There was a moment when Larry looked at Peter as if he was unsure why he was being approached by this large, genial man with a beard and benign smile. They shook hands, Larry now certain of who he was meeting. Then he turned and, politely bemused, stared at me as if I was the wrong suspect in a police identity parade.

The three of us were then prodded into an awkward line for the designated, and dreaded, 'photo opportunity'. We all had reasons to feel uncomfortable, and the three of us stared mirthlessly at the cameras in almost total embarrassment: the Past, the Present, and the Future of the National Theatre. Never did I feel history sit quite so heavily on my shoulders.

The evening proceeded as those evenings do; very emotional, very effusive, very long. The climax, and indeed the point of the evening, came at the end. Larry sat in one of the 'ashtrays' at the side of the theatre that had been named after him. The whole audience stood up, turned to him, and applauded him. He smiled, an enchanting, childlike smile of pure pleasure. He was a man for whom applause was almost better than life itself. He acknowledged the applause in a beautiful gesture, raising his right hand and turning it as if he were cupping butterflies. Joan made several attempts to lead him out but he was not going to be led. The applause went on and on. And on. The audience would happily have stayed for an hour.

On his way to the stage door, he was lured, without much protest, at least from him, through the Green Room on to a balcony above the street, still packed with a mass of fans and photographers. They shouted, whistled, applauded, and when he left he seemed to be crying, certain that this was the last time he'd hear such a sound, his life's music.

It's not necessarily that he was *the* actor of our time, he wasn't necessarily the best or the wisest or any particular superlative, even if those critical categories have any meaning at all. He simply satisfied a desire for actors to be larger than life, and to be able to be *seen* to be acting at the same time as they are moving you to tears or to laughter. It's the desire to be knowingly seduced.

He satisfied so many needs and longings both within the theatre and without. People want greatness, glory, extremes. That's why they want to go to the theatre; they want it to be bigger, more extreme, more daring, more physical than their own lives. Kafka said, perhaps unexpectedly, 'If theatre is to affect life, it must be stronger, more intense than ordinary life. That is the law of gravity.' It could be Olivier's epitaph.

Like a youth sitting round the campfire listening to the tales of the village elders, I've heard countless stories of the genesis of the National Theatre building. I've often sat late at night after a technical rehearsal with a designer puzzling over the idiosyncrasies of the design of the Olivier Theatre. There was a building committee which comprised many directors (Peter Brook, Bill Gaskill, John Dexter, Michael Eliott), and designers (Jocelyn Herbert, John Bury). All of them in recollection are unanimous about one thing: it was Larry's baby. It's not only for that reason that it's appropriate that it's named after him. It embodies him as he was – grand, grandiose even, bold, ambitious, difficult, exasperating even, but often thrilling and occasionally unique. When it works there's no auditorium in the world that is as intoxicating as the Olivier; that was as true of the actor as it is of the theatre.

To have three theatres in one building is, to say the least, a noble project. It was his will, his wilfulness, his ambition, that realised Granville-Barker, William Archer and Shaw's vision. When the National Theatre was built, a 'dream made concrete' (a metaphor made literal), Olivier was asked what he thought of it. He smiled wryly: 'It's an experiment.' Witty, I think.

I was lucky with my first outing in the Olivier Theatre. I directed *Guys and Dolls* and I've still never encountered anything as addictive as standing at the back towards the end of the show, night after night, as the audience, banked on the slopes of the auditorium like eager pilgrims, erupted like the roll of an avalanche, swamping the stage with warmth and approbation. When Larry (who had wanted to play Nathan Detroit at the Old Vic) came to see the show he was generous. He loved it. 'But the accents,' he said, 'a bit of a *mélange*.'

It's always said of Churchill that he was a man who exactly

matched the moment of history, and it's a leaden truism that we shall never see his like again; the same can be said of Olivier. It's impossible, for a catalogue of reasons to do with finance, the structure of the film industry and the theatre, the spirit of the age and the taste of the times, that we will ever again see a great buccaneering actor-manager who is also a Hollywood film star, who is equally celebrated in the theatre, and who is capable of remaking his life and his art so often and so judiciously as he did. It's said, 'Happy the land that needs no heroes.' Happier, perhaps, but duller, certainly.

PETER BROOK

When I was twenty-three, I was working as a barman, audio-typist, labourer and photographer's assistant while ostensibly being an actor. I had, however, seen Peter Brook's production of *King Lear*, and I knew there was something I wanted to do with my life: I wanted to be a theatre director.

I wrote to Brook (how I found his address I don't know) and he replied, said he didn't know how he could help me, and invited me to come and talk with him. I went to his house in Holland Park, to a large room with a pine floor, some lovely drawings and a grand piano.

We met. He talked. I listened. He spoke with great clarity, with unforced charm and without any air of talking down to me, although I was thoroughly and obviously ignorant and starstruck. Like all exceptionally intelligent people, he offered me the gift of his intelligence and required me to give my best in return. He spoke of how plays were revealed during rehearsals, not mapped out beforehand by the director, of how rehearsals must be a journey, of how there was no such thing as a definitive production; of magic, of instinct, of showmanship. I asked if I might be his assistant. 'Why?' he said. 'You're a great teacher.' 'You can only learn from yourself,' he said. 'From doing it yourself.'

I left determined to try to fit my small feet into his large footprints.

I have seen most of his work in the succeeding years. I have been exasperated as often as I have been overwhelmed, charmed

121

as often as repelled, awed as often as bored. His staging has consistently had the flair, brilliance and bravura that could be attention-seeking if it were not so obviously the consequence of trying to find the most expressive way of telling the story.

In spite of his supreme command of stage machinery, he wearied early of the 'train-set' side of theatre, what he describes as the *quincaillerie*, the 'ironmongery', of stage production. He can make the terrible isolation of a mad king alone on a brightly lit stage as much of a *coup de théâtre* as a snake of flame on a bare earth floor, twisting out of the dark, pulling a dancer in its wake.

His search for a new theatrical language culminated, in its English phase, with his production of *A Midsummer Night's Dream*. Its magic was a true 'theatre magic', effected by the performer rather than the technician. It's a paradox to many that Brook's work is always concerned with conferring authority on the performer rather than celebrating the director.

I admire what I would call, in defiance of mockery, his spiritual quest. He has often, I think courageously, laid himself open to accusations of naivety at best, pretentiousness at worst. I remember an *Aquarius* programme in which a white-robed Brook was seen at the prow of a small boat, crossing an African lake. A gnarled old man advanced towards Brook as he disembarked, arms outstretched, crying, '*Kwabo, kwabo.*' Brook embraced him and replied, '*Kwabo, kwabo.*' Years later I discovered the meaning of the haunting salutation. It was: 'Buddy, can you spare a dime?'

He has cunningly resisted being perceived as an administrator or an entrepreneur, although he has performed these roles brilliantly. When I was about to be appointed Director of the National, he said to me, 'You don't want to do that. Can't you find someone to do it for you?' Perhaps he'd found the perfect partner in Peter Hall at the RSC. 'Peter was wonderful at the memos,' he said.

Most of all I admire his refusal ever to be satisfied, ever to 'finish' a piece of work. For him theatre must always be alive and therefore always changing. I had lunch with him just after *The Mahabharata* opened in Paris, and he said he'd learned something really useful in putting on the Indian epic. I waited anxiously, fearing a gnomic riddle. 'What have you discovered?' I asked. 'Never to have a press night,' he replied. 'It stops you from going on working.'

The capacity to go on working is something for which all the directors I know envy Peter as much as they envy his talent. Something to do with his well-timed self-exile to Paris, they presume, which seems to have inoculated him against the plagues of self-doubt, the vagaries of fashion, the attrition of parochial sniping, from weariness and careerism. He seems to have managed to exempt himself from the mid-life crisis that affects theatre directors (not always in mid-life), which is something to do with a frustration at not being an '*auteur*', with repetition, constant barter and compromise, and something perhaps to do with an inability to reinvent the medium as he does. So we seek refuge in opera, in television, in musicals, in teaching, in writing, in administration – and look once again towards Peter Brook or an inspiration to return to the theatre.

A guru and a showman, he inspires me to think that the theatre is not only important, it's indispensable. I suppose that makes him a sort of hero to me.

KEN CAMPBELL

Toscanini said that when people spoke of 'great' performances they were talking of 'some fool's memory of the last bad performance'. What he meant, and expressed so biliously, is that it is hard to challenge the orthodoxy of 'great' performance. It's true that some critics have a gift for describing a performance, but however vivid their powers of description they are doomed to the status of obituarists: we don't have the originals to test against our own experience and our own taste.

Those who work in the theatre, at least most actors, do not have much interest in memorabilia or in history. They are not particularly intrigued by how the great X or Y, or even Z, played a particular part. They glory in the fact that their performance exists only in the present tense and in the future, and denies the past. The past is for the critics and the archivists. That is the joy of the medium. That is its allure, its mystery.

It's hard to subscribe to the authorised version of the 'great' performances. Either we haven't seen them or we choose to dissent. I have much admired Laurence Olivier in performances on film from *Wuthering Heights* to *Term of Trial*, and in the theatre from *Uncle Vanya* to *The Party*, but no critical catechism will make me accept that his Othello was anything more than mildly risible. And in spite of the overwhelming evidence of countless critics' polls I am unconvinced that *Citizen Kane* is the greatest film ever made. Like the 'great' performances beloved of critical orthodoxy it draws attention in every frame, however brilliant, precisely to its own brilliance. The machinery, as in a hi-tech building, is there to be marvelled at, and the heart is left unengaged.

I know what I am talking about is taste, and for my taste I have seen only one performance that I would unhesitatingly describe as 'great': that is Vanessa Redgrave as Rosalind. Beyond that I have a large catalogue of memories of vastly exciting, awesome, beguiling, and even heartbreaking performances but few that have given me as much pleasure as Ken Campbell as Professor Molereasons.

Professor Molereasons is the presiding genius of a play called *School for Clowns*, a German play for children adapted by Ken from the original by Friedrich Karl Waechter. Like many of Ken's most successful projects (or 'capers' as he'd refer to them) he's taken someone else's idea, and turned it into something inimitable.

Indeed, when it comes to expanding, developing, even appropriating other people's notions, Ken can be positively Shakespearian, if only in his resemblance to Autolycus, the 'snapper-up of unconsidered trifles'.

The play takes place in a (fairly) conventional, old-fashioned schoolroom occupied by four pupils – clowns of largely irrelevant ages and sexes, and their teacher Professor Molereasons, a remorseless advocate of discipline. The play's structure is simple: the Professor opens his large book, finds a topic for the lesson (e.g., 'Help! Help! My aeroplane's on fire!'), and instructs the clowns on how to act it out. The clowns always start according to instructions, quietly and submissively. As their invention multiplies, and their enthusiasms grow, anarchy invariably brings on the intervention of the increasingly desperate Molereasons: 'SILENCE, CLOWNS!! I AM UNABLE TO CONTINUE IN THESE CIRCUMSTANCES!!' His final threat is to leave the room, aware even as he does so of the painful weakness of this sanction. There is no teacher alive, and no child, who would fail to recognise the dilemma.

The play is as fine a metaphor as one can find for teaching, for learning, for the relationship of pupil and teacher, and for the connections between comedy, anarchy, and childhood. When Ken did the play at Nottingham Playhouse, we had just opened Trevor

Griffith's *Comedians*, which, as Ken observed, was *School for Clowns* for grown-ups.

In fact Ken's work has always appealed to the child in me: anarchic, naughty, unreverential, silly even. When I started as Director of Nottingham Playhouse it was more or less mandatory to pay homage to the local history of your 'community'. I had little taste for a dramatised documentary about laceworkers, and even less for a revisionist version of the Robin Hood story. I had heard about a little-known local hero called Bendigo, a prize fighter who was once champion of England, and I asked Ken, who conscripted his friends Dave Hill and Andy Andrews, to dramatise the life of the boxer.

Ken was intrigued by his training methods. Bendigo used to go into pubs and spit in people's beer to annoy them, which would, unsurprisingly, provoke a fight. He once did it to a dancer who pranced about so much that Bendigo couldn't hit him, thus giving him the key to his distinctive, prancing style. In Ken's show *Bendigo: The Little Known Facts* his inspiration to become a boxer came from his mother who, taunted beyond endurance by his indolence, flattened him with a rolling pin. He responded by thumping her with a powerful straight left. 'Ah son,' she said, ''tis a metaphor surely of your life to be.'

I thought this show one of the most enjoyable things I had ever seen in the theatre. So did many of the audience, but not the man who Ken overheard in an interval say to his wife, 'I can't imagine the sort of person who would enjoy this stuff.' He presumably didn't return the following year when we staged another item of little-known local history based on the folk myth of the Nottinghamshire village of Gotham where the villagers discovered, round about the Middle Ages, that if they were declared insane they were exempt from the Poll Tax. Prescience indeed.

The show was called *Walking Like Geoffrey* and involved the villagers being taught to act silly by the village half-wit, Geoffrey, and a plot that went backwards in time, the complexity of which would have done credit to Tolkien. The evening reached its climax in a mass demonstration of eccentric walking from the school of Max Wall for the benefit of the Tax Man. He was driven from the village into insanity.

Shortly before he defected to an academic job in Canada the excellent Ronald Bryden, then critic of the *Observer*, wrote of *Walking Like Geoffrey*: 'If there's a future for British theatre it must lie here.' I wish I knew where it had all gone. More and more I find myself defending the theatre or proselytising for it as more and more people find excuses for not liking the medium or just not going out. We're made to feel like coracle makers or Morris dancers: participants in an archaic ritual performed only for the benefit of the devotees. Another review of the show was less generous. It objected to almost everything about it, and in particular to the intrusive laughter of what the critic took to be friends of the authors. Ken was outraged. 'What does he mean, friends, we *are* the bloody authors!'

There was a sketch from the show that Ken decided years later to perform at an Amnesty International concert at Drury Lane. Somewhat against my will I agreed to direct the piece again. It involved the death of an Elizabethan nobleman trying to cheat his destiny by breaking through the 'warp and weft of time': setting up a situation in which time passed quickly (pleasure) and time passed slowly (pain). Running between besmocked wenches and nagging wife he failed to make the 'thread of marching time elastic' and died through a surfeit of blank verse. Or as Ken said, 'Death by RADA breathing.'

At Drury Lane Ken decided there had to be an extra ingredient to lard the nightmare of the dying time-traveller: live pigs. This was not a success. I don't mind working with children, and some animals can be perfectly docile, but take my advice: stay away from pigs. They aren't happy in theatres, and have the most disturbing ways of showing their unhappiness. I can hear their cries of distress to this day.

Most of Ken's capers look as if they are going to be follies and turn out to be inspired gestures of showmanship. *The Road Show*, like its subject matter – the dramatisation of pub myths and tall stories – eventually became a part of theatrical folklore. *The Warp*, a day-long play that I first saw in the Liverpool Theatre of Science Fiction, I would rank beside *The Wars of the Roses* and *The Oresteia* as great theatre. It's as ambitious, as long, and certainly as entertaining as *The Ring*. I was offered a job in *The Warp*. 'Peter Hall's turned it down,' said Ken. 'It's the part of the man who wants to run the world. It's not bad, you're only on for three minutes.' I regret not doing that as much as I regret declining the offer by a friend, a performance artist, to make love in public at the Round House in 1967, while wired to a microphone, an ECT machine, and a TV camera.

I would very happily see again *Pilk's Madhouse*, the confessions of an apparently genuine sage who Ken had invented in Canada, and *The Strange Case of Charles Dexter Ward*, an opera of sorts, and *The Great Caper*, a play of sorts. These shows made me feel that there was no place on earth where I could be experiencing quite this heady sense of delight in the preposterousness, the invention, the wit and the energy that was on offer.

There are two sequels to *School for Clowns*: *Clowns on a School Outing*, and *Peef*. They should ideally be performed on the same day by the same actors, in a sort of clownfest. Ideally they would feature Ken as Professor Molereasons, but it would be wiser not to let him direct the plays. I once saw a rehearsal of his where an actor who had failed to provide the necessary energy and invention to satisfy Ken was hurled against the wall with Ken screaming in his all too idiosyncratic voice, like an exhaust pipe with a broken silencer, 'Act PROPER!'

Ken's evangelism, his enthusiasms of the moment, can sometimes be hard to endure, particularly on the phone at one o'clock in the morning: Gerry Webb of Space Consultancy and Interplanetary travel, EST, Max Wall, Spike Jones, Ian Dury, Charles Fort (the visionary), Robert McKee the script doctor, the Royal Dickens Theatre, the underwater show in the Liverpool swimming pool, the office on the Essex marshes, Werner the dog . . . There is no one who seizes the moment with quite so much enthusiasm and is quite so relentless in wanting to share it with others.

He once graphically displayed to me the two sides of his character, holding a hand in front of each half of his face in turn: the pirate and the char. The pirate is wild, sometimes savage, sometimes bullying, ambitious, brazen, loud. The char is mournful and melancholic, and sometimes, though not very often, quite tender.

In 1900, in Paris, there was a prize called the Guzmann Prize: 100,000 F for anyone who could communicate with an extra-terrestrial being on another planet. The planet Mars was excluded on the grounds that it was too easy to communicate with Martians. I think Ken should, belatedly, be offered this prize. He told me of an encounter he'd once had with the Venusian Consul in London; I suspect he was talking about himself. He'd been sent here to shake up our ideas about theatre. I hope he's still working for them.

IAN CHARLESON

I didn't know Ian well until I worked with him on *Guys and Dolls* in 1982. I knew him then as an actor of charm, of wit, of skill, with a kind of engaging melancholy of the Mastroianni variety, which he could dispel with a sardonic and self-mocking wit. He often looked truly beautiful, even angelic; then a mischievous smile would appear and all thoughts of angels would fly away like frightened starlings.

I'd offered him the part in *Guys and Dolls* on the basis of his acting and hearing him sing at parties. It was typical of him that he insisted on singing the score for me before he accepted the part, and equally typical that when he'd finished singing he said to me, 'You enjoyed that, didn't you, Richard?' He knew he could make an audience (and a director) cry with a romantic ballad, and he loved to do just that as much as he loved to torment me with his relentless mockery of my attempts to dance alongside the cast.

He was a fine, light, unfailingly truthful romantic actor, something that the French value more than we do. Like Cary Grant, he had the gift of making the difficult look effortlessly simple. But with Brick in *Cat on a Hot Tin Roof* and with his Hamlet, he discovered a new gravity. He became, in my view, a real heavyweight.

We had talked some time ago about the parts that he desperately wanted to play – Richard II, Angelo, Benedick, and Hamlet and – as he said to me – 'Lear, God willing.' He had a real passion for Shakespeare, rather rare in his generation. He really loved the density of thought, the great Shakespearian paradoxes, the lyricism, the energy of the verse. He didn't want to paraphrase it; the meaning was for him in the poetry and the poetry in the meaning.

When I asked him to play Hamlet I knew he'd been ill, had even had pneumonia, and that he still had a chronic sinus complaint which gave him large, swollen bags under his eyes. On bad days it was barely possible to glimpse the face beneath the swelling, a malicious parody of his beauty. He was without vanity, but not without hope. He told me that he was HIV Positive and that he thought that the eyes would respond to treatment. When we embarked on rehearsals he was having regular, and immensely painful, acupuncture treatment, and later on, chemotherapy which exhausted and debilitated him. Later in his illness he defiantly rejected all treatment; he wanted to be himself, however painful that was.

About halfway through the rehearsal period we discussed the future – an unspecified projection. 'Do you think I can go on as Hamlet looking like this?' he said. 'You'll get better,' I said. 'We have to be positive,' he said. And we were. Our text was, of course, from *Hamlet*:

There's nothing either good or bad but thinking makes it so.

Hamlet is a poem of death. It charts one of the great human rites of passage – from immaturity to accommodation with death. Hamlet grows up, in effect, to grow dead. Until he leaves for England ('From this time forth/ My thoughts be bloody or be nothing worth') he is on a reckless helter-skelter swerving between reason and chaos. When he returns from England he is changed, aged, matured, reconciled somehow to his end. We see Hamlet in a graveyard obsessed with the physical consequences of death, and then in a scene with Horatio prior to the duel he talks to him about his premonition of death:

. . . thou wouldst not think how ill all's here about my heart. But it is no matter . . . it is but foolery . . . We defy augury. There is a special providence in the fall of a sparrow. If it be now, it is not to come; if it be not to come, it will be now; if it be not now, yet it will come. The readiness is all. Since no man of aught he leaves knows aught, what is't to leave betimes? Let be.

We talked a great deal about Hamlet's accommodation with death, always as a philosophical proposition, his own state lurking just below the surface, hidden subtext. Ian was very fastidious about the 'Let be'. It wasn't, for him, a chiding of Horatio, or a shrug of stoic indifference, it was an assertion, a proposed epitaph, perhaps: don't fuss, don't panic, don't be afraid.

I've no idea if it was Kennedy's coinage, more likely one of his speech-writer's, but the definition of courage as 'grace under pressure' was perfectly suited to Ian. It was something more than stoicism. He defied his illness with a spirit that was dazzling, quite without self-pity, self-dramatisation, and at least openly, without despair. During rehearsals he was utterly without reserve. Where there had been a kind of detachment or caution, a 'Scottishness', perhaps, there was a deep well of generosity, of affection – a largeness of heart, and the only 'Scottish' characteristics that he showed were his doggedness and his persistence.

In his last performance of *Hamlet* he acted as if he knew that it was the last time he'd be on stage. He'd had flu and hadn't played the previous two nights; he was feeling guilty about what he saw as his lack of professionalism. 'If they pay you, you should turn up,' he said. His performance on that Monday night was like watching a man who had been rehearsing for playing Hamlet all his life. He wasn't playing the part, he became it. By the end of the performance he was visibly exhausted, each line of his final scene painfully wrung from him, his farewell and the character's agonisingly merged. He stood at the curtain call like a tired boxer, battered by applause.

When he became unable to perform, it was a real deprivation to him. Without that there was nothing to hang on to. 'You know me, Richard, if there are two people out there who I can impress, I'd be there if I could.' And he would, if he'd had the strength. We're often accused of sentimentality in the theatre, but it can't be sentimental to miss terribly someone whose company gave so much joy, whose talent really *did* add to the sum of human happiness, and whose courage was beyond admiration.

I had a letter from him a few weeks before he died, just before Christmas. He said:

One day when I'm better I'd love to attempt Hamlet again, and all the rest; and together we can revitalise Shakespeare. Anyway I hope this is not a dream and I can't tell you how much of a kick I got out of doing the part, if only for the short time I could . . .

Let be.

ION CARAMITRU

They used to call pig's trotters patriots in Bucharest butchers' shops; they were the only part of the animal that hadn't gone abroad in Ceauşescu's drive for foreign exchange. What the pigs left behind was a country close to famine, frozen in a Stalinist time warp like a mammoth in a glacier. If the British response to hardship is to maintain a stiff upper lip, the Romanian approach is '*haz de necaz*' – to get fun out of tragedy. They've had ample opportunity to put this to the test in the last forty-five years.

I got to know Romania through its theatre, which I first encountered at the Edinburgh Festival in 1971. The Bulandra Company from Bucharest was presenting two plays at the Lyceum Theatre: *Carnival Scenes* by the Romanian playwright I.L. Carigiale, and *Leonce and Lena* by Buchner. The two productions exemplified the best of Romanian theatre. Carigiale is a writer described (by Irving Wardle) as a cross between Labiche and Gogol – witty, satirical, robust, farcical, energetic and humane. None of these characteristics is specifically Romanian, but the combination is distinctly so. The productions and the acting had an engaging, droll, and highly charged charm; and outstanding in a cast of richly talented and idiosyncratic actors was a young man described by Michael Billington as the most exciting young actor he'd seen since the debut of Ian McKellen.

In the following years I came to know Ion Caramitru and the work of the Bulandra Company well. The company was started in 1948 by Lucia Bulandra, who was like Olivier in combining a great acting talent with a formidable ability as a manager and talent spotter. She remained director until her death in 1965. Her funeral was a great public event. So many people turned out on the streets for the procession of the body from the theatre to the cemetery that the pallbearers (who included the young Caramitru) were jostled, shaking the body. Her head nodded from side to side, indicating, as in life, that the answer to whatever they wanted was 'No'.

She had, however, said 'Yes' to the appointment of her successor, Livie Ciulei. Ciulei presided over the company from 1965 until his dismissal in 1973. (He emigrated in 1979, becoming Director of the Guthrie Theatre in Minneapolis.) Under his direction the Bulandra went through a golden period, gaining a well-deserved international reputation. An uneasy relationship between the successful, but highly individualistic, company and the Cultural Ministry exploded in 1973.

A production of *The Government Inspector* was banned by the Ministry after three performances. The 'special ideological forces' of the Ministry, encouraged by their Russian colleagues, saw the production as unequivocally anti-government and anti-Russian. Gogol's stage direction at the end – 'a frozen tableau of consterna-tion' – had been staged as an endlessly repeating whirl of robotlike bureaucrats stumbling about the stage in an ever-growing fog. The director, Lucian Pintilei, lost the right to work and emigrated. Ciulei was sacked; some leading actors lost their responsibilities within the administration, and an era of numbing censorship was ushered in. This was merely an echo of the repression happening on the larger, political, stage. The repertoire now had to be approved by the Councillor of Culture and Social Education, individual plays unknown to the Councillor had to be submitted a year in advance, and a special committee of twenty-five bureaucrats attended special previews. The most effective form of censorship, and one that is not unknown in the West, was the gradual diminution of subsidy. In the last two years before the Revolution the company existed on a sub-sidy of less than one tenth of their subsidy at the beginning of the seventies. There was barely enough money to pay the actors, and none for the heating and electricity.

I visited Romania several times in the seventies. By the end of the decade Ion Caramitru had become a leading actor and the Deputy Director of the company (the Director was a place man; a Party member and a dull actor to boot), and in 1982 on a visit to London he invited me to direct a play for the Bulandra. I suggested *Hamlet*, partly because it seemed an excellent part for Caramitru, and partly because it seemed an all too appropriate play for Romania. I went to Bucharest in 1983 to cast the play and talk to the prospective designer. The city had changed since I was there a few years earlier. Armed with images from *The Balkan Trilogy* of Olivia Manning, I had not been disappointed on my first visit; a city of wide boulevards, elegant and humanely proportioned *fin de siècle* houses often decorated with florid and flamboyant art nouveau features, and populated with a Latin people who bore their oppression with a beguiling mixture of diffidence and discreet subversion.

The Bucharest I encountered in 1983 was a drab parody of its former self. It had been harmed more by Ceauşescu than by the recent earthquake. Obdurate and systematic neglect and deprivation darkened the face of the city; at night literally so for all the street lights and shop windows were extinguished in a misplaced scheme to save energy for industry. The downward spiral continued during the eighties. After ten o'clock a curfew was effectively introduced. Cinemas, restaurants, theatres were obliged to close and 'night clubs', with a wonderfully absurd magnanimity, were allowed to open between eight and ten.

If I had any doubts about whether *Hamlet* was the appropriate play, I was given ample confirmation of its suitability. Bugged telephones and hotel rooms, the ever-present Securitate, the smug strutting arrogance of the Party's apparatchiks, the friends who lowered their voices and looked about them before speaking, the fear of prison and the familiarity with those who had experienced it, the swaggering display of the privileges of the Nomeklatura; in short, it was Elsinor.

I was finally unable to do the production and was replaced by a gifted young Romanian, Alex Tocilescu. For about nine months he, a brace of poets, five actors, and a novelist worked to achieve a translation that they felt was true to Shakespeare and to the condition of Romania. The Ministry had accepted the idea of *Hamlet* until the ideological committee attended a preview. They found the translation too 'modern', too 'close', and the production too provocative. Caramitru came very near to an explosive confrontation with the Ministry: 'You can't stop Shakespeare, or at least you can't be seen to.' Surprisingly the appeal worked, the fear of becoming the laughing stock of the world outweighed the fear of inciting unhealthy thoughts.

The production opened triumphantly in 1985 and played two hundred performances through the hardest years of the regime. Ceauşescu had graduated from being a malign clown to a psychotic ogre. His *folies de grandeur* consisted of rasing villages to the ground in order to rehouse peasants in tower blocks, sweeping aside boulevards because the streets from his residence to his office were insufficiently straight, building miles of preposterously baroque apartment blocks which echoed in concrete the lines of Securitate men standing beneath them, and led the eye towards a gigantic palace which made Stalin's taste in architecture look restrained. They ran out of marble to clad the walls and the floors, and had to invent a process to make a synthetic substitute out of marble dust; and there was never enough gold for all the door handles of the hundreds of rooms, or the taps of the scores of bathrooms. It was a palace of Oz, built for a demented wizard, costing the lives of hundreds of building workers who, numbed by cold, fell from the flimsy scaffolding and were brushed away like rubble, to be laid out in a room reserved solely for the coffins of the expendable workforce. There was a photograph of Ceauşescu that showed only one ear, and there's a Romanian saying that to have one ear is to be mad. So another ear was painstakingly painted on the official photograph. Such are the ways of great men. I went to a conference in Bucharest after the Revolution. I was asked, 'What is the difference between Alexander the Great and the Buddha?' I had no answer.

The Bulandra Company had suffered, like the country as a whole, from a decimation of its resources, a crippling of morale, and a defection of talent (mostly directors). There was, however, one ironic gain. As the regime tightened its grip and the corrosive effect of tyranny leaked into every area of public and private life, the theatre gathered more and more power as the sole public medium of expression where thoughts could be spoken, ideas asserted, passions voiced, through allegory and metaphor. The code was one that could be read by an audience but not challenged by the censors. When I saw *Hamlet* in Bucharest I was seeing a play whose resonances were, literally, painfully telling. Hamlet was seen unambiguously as a man fighting against Claudius/Ceauşescu, and, if he vacillated, accused himself of cowardice, cursed himself for his inaction, it only reflected the audience's awareness of their own frailty. They sat enraptured in an unheated theatre for several hours on uncomfortable seats or crouched on the edge of the stage, swathed in scarves and overcoats. Line after line was greeted with the applause of recognition; this was their story.

Ion Caramitru was in London in December 1989 to give a poetry reading at the Barbican to celebrate the centenary of the celebrated Romanian poet, Eminescu. We spoke a lot about recent events in Eastern Europe. 'The Berlin Wall has moved to the Romanian border. There won't be any changes in Romania.' We're all prophets with hindsight. I ruefully said goodbye to him, promising to visit an unchanged Romania during the next year.

He returned to Bucharest on the 13th of December. There were reports of unrest in Timişoara on the 16th of December, but no one in Bucharest knew what had happened. Ion had to go to Cluj, in the north, to give a talk. While he was there he heard rumours of a massacre in Timişoara, flew back to Bucharest and found Ceauşescu on the TV at the airport speaking from a balcony to a huge crowd. Suddenly the TV broadcast stopped. Ion left the airport but could barely drive his car for the crush of coaches filled with riot police heading for the centre. He joined the crowd and the square was surrounded by soldiers and Securitate. Ion was recognised by students and teenagers, who asked him to help them persuade people to join the opposition. The Securitate were infiltrating the crowd as he enlisted support and gave encouragement. 'It was the beginning of a new world,' he said.

The next morning there were opposition slogans in office buildings, groups of people emerging all over the city. By ten o'clock it was known that the Commander of the Army had either committed suicide or had been executed. The soldiers embraced the people, and the Securitate started to fight. Hundreds of protesters were killed. Two months later you could still see where they died. In squares, on pavements, on street corners, in shop doorways, you could see small clusters of candles and bunches of flowers. Often they described the outline of a body and they haunt the memory like the shadows of the vaporised bodies in Hiroshima.

Nobody knew what to do. Nobody knew where to go. There was no order, no plan. They saw Ceauşescu's helicopter overhead, leaflets were scattered from it. They read: 'DON'T LISTEN TO FOREIGNERS'.

Finding himself with a group near the TV station, Ion suggested that they take it over. A general said to him, 'My army is at your disposal. Tell us where to go.' Heady stuff for an actor. And off they went. There was fierce fighting round the TV station, but by the time Ion went in the crowd parted for him and he found the TV station guarded by only one Securitate man, who was trembling too much even to raise his hand in a salute.

'Then we opened a programme, but it was the same announcer who had been broadcasting all these lies for YEARS. So I said no. But the TV people said yes, let him speak. We are all guilty. I told him to apologise for his past. He did and then I went on and I said we're free, we've won. God was with us. Don't shoot anyone. Join us . . . I was too full of emotion to speak properly.'

After two or three hours Iliescu, Roman and Brucan arrived at the TV station. They decided to form a provisional government; a hundred or so dissidents, poets, artists, and teachers joined the National Salvation Front. Ion became one of the twelve-man Executive Committee. He was the only one who had not been a member of the Party. The promise of the NSF was to administrate the country until elections could be held; it was never intended to become a political party in itself. This was one of many broken promises. On the night of the 23rd of December, Ion tried to persuade Iliescu to go out on the balcony in front of the huge crowd, tear up his Party card and scatter the pieces in the wind; a simple theatrical gesture that could have changed the history of his government.

Ion fought his corner in the Provisional Government as Vice-President with responsibility for culture and education, and when the elections were announced he stood as an independent. Like all the other independents (with the exception of Andrez Plezu, who succeeded him as Minister of Culture), he failed to get elected. Many tried to persuade him to stand for President, and there is no doubt that he had a following that would flatter any politician. He refused, and decided to return to the theatre to become head of a newly formed Theatre Union, dedicated to getting revolution off the streets and into the revival of theatres. Perhaps Madame Bulandra was shaking her head at her protégé, fearful that a gain for politics would be a loss to the theatre, and I'm sure that no theatre could afford to lose the services of this wry, talented, intelligent and humane actor.

To be involved in a revolution is to take theatre to the streets. The difficulties that theatres face in Romania are a microcosm of the difficulties faced by the government: to rebuild a culture debilitated by years of deprivation and neglect. They need any help they can get.

It's been a depressing sight to see the Romanian government

blundering into folly after folly, the Western governments withdrawing aid, and the public withdrawing their fickle affections, when the sunburst of revolution gives way to the grey light of day. There used to be a giant statue of Lenin in front of the huge Stalinist wedding cake of the Ministry of Culture. It was torn down during the Revolution. A small placard was put in its place on the graffiti-covered granite plinth. It said: 'GOD HELP ROMANIA.' We could do our bit too.

TONY HARRISON

I was driving through France recently discussing the French for roof-rack (*le roofrack*, recently dehyphenated). In addition to *le roofrack* we would need, I said, some *corde* and possibly (showing off now) *une amarre*. 'What's that?' said a sceptical wife. 'A hawser,' I replied. 'Hawser? Hawser?' she ruminated. 'That's a Tony Harrison word.' And together, like infants learning *Hiawatha*, we chanted from *v.*:

When the hawser of the blood-tie's hacked, or frays . . .

It's as characteristic a Harrison line as one could find: rhythmic, memorable, muscled, alliterative, dramatic and impenitently English.

It's one of the many paradoxes, the v's if you like, of Tony's work that his is such a recognisably English voice; not a metaphorical 'voice', but a sound that, once you have met its author, unforgettably animates the poetry on the page and dramatises it when he reads it aloud. It's not Received Pronunciation (against which he rails evangelically), nor the fluting sound of college common-rooms or cathedral cloisters, it's not dry, muted or ascetic. It's musical, sensual, working-class and Yorkshire. It's not a professional Yorkshire voice that speaks from an ersatz tradition of thee-the-beery-bloky defiant little Englanders, but a voice with a sense of place and class. A heartland from which the speaker has been separated.

The baker's son from Leeds is probably the most cosmopolitan man I know. Multilingual (Greek, ancient and modern, Latin, Italian, French, Czech and Hausa), much travelled – a citizen, as they say, of the world – living, often rather precariously, between London, Florida, New York and Newcastle. An expert in many cultures, with a curiosity about many others. Fastidiously knowledgeable about food, wine, music and the theatre. Tender, witty, wry, volatile, living up (or down) to the Yorkshire stereotype only in his rare but formidable stubbornness and intransigence.

The man is the work. It is not so much that it is autobiographical (though much of it is) but that the content invariably dramatises the ambivalences at the heart of his character and attempts to reconcile them. Tony does not deal in the familiar English mode of elipsis and reticence, but in an unremittingly direct address that is at times almost unnerving. Those opposite valencies that he invokes in *v.* are not a poet's conceits but are the syntax of his daily life – heart/brain, soul/body, male/female, family, freedom, class, culture; this is the divided territory in which he searches for harmony and despairs at its elusiveness.

I don't know if despair is his constant companion; melancholy certainly is. More than once I've heard him say that if it weren't for his ability to write he would go mad, that writing is a way of expressing, of reducing, of controlling, thoughts and feelings that would otherwise spray into chaos. It was, appropriately, the author of *The Anatomy of Melancholy* who said that all poets are mad. Perhaps without their poetry they would be.

For all this, Tony is a cheerful companion and a highly organised and practical professional man. He is, after all, as well as a poet, a playwright and a director – both disciplines that give short shrift to the dilettante. As a writer he is as methodical as any writer I know. He collects and collates information about subjects that attract him in a series of quarto-sized notebooks with quotations, newspaper cuttings, photographs, ideas, fragments of lines, all laid out meticulously. The Japanese film director Ozu used to go to his country cottage for weeks to write his scripts. When he emerged he described the script in terms of the number of cases of sake he's had to consume to write it. With Tony it's notebooks.

The notebooks contain, among other things, a continent of information about Greek drama on which he is unquestionably an absolute authority and about which he is a zealot. He has little patience with the dabblers in the Greek repertoire, or, indeed, with any form of cultural tourism. It might be argued that as a theatrical practitioner he is himself merely an enthusiastic amateur. This is not so; for many years as a translator (*Le Misanthrope, Phaedra Britannica, The Oresteia*), and as a co-author (*The Mysteries*) he has not only closely observed the processes of theatre-making but has been at times a *de facto* co-director, and as a director and author (*Trackers* and *Square Rounds*) he has a real understanding of the singularity of the medium – an acute sense of space and of language.

He is wearied but patient with the aspects of the job that often make you feel like a night-nurse, dispensing comfort, advice, treatment and solace to actors while wondering why they don't just *do* it. There are few directors, however, who are more conscientious in ensuring that the minds of the actors are concentrated with an almost religious rigour on their performance. He is the only director I know who (in *Trackers*) invites the cast to drink champagne from a three-thousand-year-old cup before going on stage.

In his poetry and his plays the sense of rhythm is as important as the meaning. Dramatic language without the sinew of rhythmic pulse is completely inert to him, and he can be violent and unforgiving about performances and productions of verse plays where the actors and directors have been deaf to the beat of the poetry. You should be able to feel the language, to taste it, to conscript the whole body as well as the mind and the mouth to savour it.

In the same way Tony wants the whole body of society, not just its head, to be involved in art. He wants art and literature to be accessible to everyone, for the distinction between high and low art to be annulled, and for art to be removed from the clutches of class distinction. However, his hatred for the pap of popular culture is almost boundless. He has a committed loathing for the propagators and purveyors of this pap and, in spite of his determined compassion, for the consumers as well. He's a populist in the same sense as Chekhov who, when told by a Narodnik actor that Gogol needed to be brought down to the level of the people, said that the problem was rather that the people needed to be brought up to the level of Gogol. If ever there was an anthem set to this theme it is *v.*

In Russia they used to kill their poets *pour encourager les autres.* The reward for the English poet is at best indifference and at worst becoming Poet Laureate. With *v.* Tony violated both ends of that spectrum. Whatever was invoked by that poem it was not indifference. Indignation, outrage, joy, sorrow, pity, perhaps, and paradoxically for a man who would violently shun any form of honour, he became the uncrowned Poet Laureate – a truly public poet.

Poets who read their work in public can often be maddeningly diffident and awkward. Tony is not of this school. He is a poet who performs rather than reads, without self-regard and without self-indulgence, and without the spurious 'performance' values that actors often bring to the reading of poetry. He does not, however, neglect the demands of volume and articulation, the sense of the event, and the awareness of his audience. He is metrically, unnervingly constant. When we were filming *v.* you could have set a metronome at the beginning of the performance and forty minutes later the poet would still have been in sync with it. In addition, he could accommodate with an actor's instinct instructions about camera movements and eyelines. He could, as we say, 'take direction'.

I first became aware of the rumbling storm provoked by Channel 4's intention to show the film of *v.* when I was making another film that also provoked severe climatic disturbances, *Tumbledown.* There were similarities in the response to both films. In both cases, before the transmission, in fact before anyone even on the production team had seen the finished films, there was a chorus of outrage, misrepresentation, prejudice, insult, bullying and condescension from MPs, journalists, peers and pundits.

Popular newspapers, as ever, found rich resources of moral indignation. I was standing in a North London car-park one grey dawn, waiting for the day's filming to begin, when a cheery make-up assistant thrust a copy of the *Daily Mail* into my hand. 'You've made the front page,' she said. I read, and I hope to give full value to the pungent prose: 'FOUR LETTER TV POEM FURY!' Only with hindsight was I grateful to the *Mail* and their even more downmarket clones for having unwittingly brought to the poem an audience whose size could never have been imagined without their gift of free publicity. It was an audience that largely came to the poem out of curiosity and was surprised to find that, not only could they understand it, but they were moved, amused, even educated by it.

The film's editor was a man who, like many victims of our educational system, had been turned off poetry at an early age. 'It was not for me,' he said. One of the greatest pleasures of making the film was watching Ray become drawn into the poem so that he felt each nuance, each rhyme, each rhythm, each shift of thought with an ever-increasing vividness. Indeed, all of us involved in making the film became evangelistic in support of the poem – its way of yoking sophisticated and ambitious philosophical speculation to minute physical observations; its astonishing variety contained within an unvarying scheme of rhyme and scansion; its pessimism as much as its optimism; and above all, its endless celebration of what it wouldn't be too grand to call the human condition. We all thought, as Ray put it, that the poem was fucking amazing. I still do, and when Tony told me that a parents' action group had succeeded in persuading the Manchester Education Committee (via the office of that renowned figure of the new enlightenment, Chief Constable James Anderton) to withdraw his poetry from the school curriculum, I felt once again that, as in Russia, poetry was dangerous. The Russian poet Gumilyov

TONY HARRISON

(who was shot) said that dead words smell bad. These are the words of the acknowledged legislators of our world who proscribe, censor, inhibit and monitor what we should read and see, and, by implication, think and feel.

If I had the slightest influence over educational policy in this country, I'd see that *v.* was a set text in every school, but of course if we lived in that sort of country, the poem wouldn't have needed to be written.

When I became Director of the National Theatre, I asked Tony what I should do there. 'Improve the wine,' he said. (As it turned out, rather more difficult than changing the repertoire.) We were having dinner a few days afterwards, several of us, a smallish room in a restaurant. Tony had, of course, ordered the wine. Lots of it. On the wall behind my head was a small etching of Andrew Marvell, which Tony caught sight of. He started to recite 'To His Coy Mistress'. One Yorkshire poet speaking through another, the intervening centuries becoming transparent. There was an almost palpable silence in the room: the air suspended. It was moving, funny, soulful, inspired by what Lorca called *duende*. 'The magical quality of a poem,' said Lorca, 'consists in it always being possessed by the *duende* so that whoever beholds it is baptised by dark water.' It's that dark water that Tony is immersed in and he wants to take us with him, sink or swim.

PLAYS

GUYS AND DOLLS

I discovered *Guys and Dolls* through my father's overcoat. It was a loudish, belted, check coat with giant shoulders, called Big Nig. 'Why is your coat called Big Nig?' I asked my father at the age of twelve. 'Read more than somewhat and you'll find out.' I already read more than somewhat, in fact my eyes ached from reading in torchlight under the bed-covers. '*More Than Somewhat!*' he growled, 'by Damon Runyon.' So I read Damon Runyon, and I understood: Big Nig was a crapshooter and Damon Runyon was a magical writer. About the same time the film of *Guys and Dolls* was released, a film based, according to the feed-box noise, on a story by Damon Runyon. I worshipped Brando, I was in love with Jean Simmons, I was cool to Sinatra, and I was entranced by the songs and the dialogue – some of which I could even recognise from the original.

In the subsequent years I came to know the Broadway cast recording well, and had a nodding acquaintance with the script. While I was at Nottingham Playhouse I'd occasionally think about doing the show and then, daunted by the demands of the score and the book, think again. I never saw a stage production until my own – not even the 1979 Half Moon Theatre production, whose director told me that *Guys and Dolls* was so good not even a director could mess it up.

In the middle of 1981 I agreed to join the National Theatre as an associate director. I had no clear programme of plays, and my first production was to be in the Olivier Theatre. Peter Hall was clearly apprehensive that I would be passionate to direct *Woyzek*, or a minor Ostrovsky, when what he needed at the time was a full-blooded crowd-pleaser. 'Could you think,' he asked plaintively, 'of doing a major popular classic?'

I thought, but came up with nothing until I stood in a record shop in Dean Street, which specialised in Broadway show-albums and Ennio Morricone film scores. I saw the title *Guys and Dolls*, and knew that I was being given a nudge. I told Peter Hall, who was cautious but enthusiastic. I was, he said, the latest in a long line of claimants who had wanted to direct it at the National – including Olivier, who had planned to do the show at the Old Vic in 1970. He had cast it – himself as Nathan, Geraldine McEwan as Adelaide, Edward Woodward as Sky, and Louise Purnell as Sarah, and dance rehearsals had begun; his coronary thrombosis nipped the production in the bud. Olivier always credited Ken Tynan with initiating the idea of doing *Guys and Dolls*, and my own adult enthusiasm owes a lot to Tynan's advocacy. He described it as the 'second best American play' – the best being *Death of a Salesman*.

Peter gave the go-ahead in early October – we had three months to cast and design the show before rehearsals started in January. I had directed musicals before but never on the scale that we anticipated in the Olivier; it seemed like moving from a back-garden paddling pool to the Pacific Ocean. I started work with John Gunter, the designer, in mid-October. We had worked together intermittently for about as long as Nathan Detroit and Adelaide had been engaged, and we communicated by then in a sort of shorthand. Soon John began to develop a scheme for the show. We realised our choices were simple – to opt for a standing set that would embrace all locations, with a production that laid little emphasis on the traditional values of the Broadway musical; or to go for broke – epic, flamboyant, extravert and spectacular, Broadway in its heyday.

We talked a lot about movies – the fluency with which Gene Kelly's films blended the conventions of studio naturalism with extreme fantasy; the affectation, parody and bravura of Scorsese's *New York, New York*; the visual hallmarks of gangster movies. We discussed each scene in terms of staging it in a film version, and then translated those ideas into the appropriate gestures for the giant jaws of the Olivier stage. We failed to persuade Peter Hall to allow us a 'research' trip to New York, but we drew very heavily on Andreas Feininger's wonderful photographs of Manhattan in the forties. John began to create a structure that suggested Times Square by day. For night, we thought idly of neon – impractical, we thought, too bright.

I went for a weekend in Paris, and in the bookshop in the Beauborg Centre I saw an American book: *Let There Be Neon* by Rudi Stera. I lost no time in telling John that divine intervention had occurred. The book is a loving account of the birth, history, manufacture and current use of neon. We became entranced with it. 'Neon is writing with light,' said Rudi Stera, and John began to write with it. The set he designed was a joyous and ingenious invention that fully exploited the most thrilling aspect of stage design – the ability to transform space; it moved effortlessly from the intimate to the epic, from the realistic to the fantastic, while making each location specific and detailed and full of character.

Sue Blane, the costume designer, matched John's invention and joined us, along with David Toguri, the choreographer, in long, discursive planning meetings. Sometimes we sat in silence; sometimes we chattered like parrots, and sometimes speculated ruminatively: 'What if we were to do . . .' followed by a pregnant silence. We were much preoccupied by the low dive in Havana. At one stage we decided to have a café entirely populated by émigrés from films set in Cuba – Humphrey Bogart, Lauren Bacall, Carmen Miranda, Sydney Greenstreet, Spencer Tracy – even the young Fidel Castro. We settled for a drag queen and eccentric local clientele.

To have the talents of John Gunter, David Toguri, Sue Blane, and David Hersey (the lighting designer) was luck of a rare degree, but when it came to casting it was clear the production had a charmed life. Casting is a lottery; it's an invariable law of casting that the actor or actress you want has just signed for a film, or two years with the RSC, or is planning to have a baby. In this case it seemed as if destiny had marked the actors' cards, and within a short time we had Julia McKenzie, Bob Hoskins, Ian Charleson, Julie Covington and a company of great individual and collective strength. 'We want people with bumps,' said Cy Feuer, the producer of the original *Guys and Dolls* production. Our cast was richly corrugated.

All musicals are love stories; *Guys and Dolls* is endowed with two of them. It's a 'fairy-tale of New York', peopled by many of Damon Runyon's characters but without the savage undertow of most of his stories – more Runyonesque than Runyonese. His world is a wholly successful fictional creation, as hermetic, consistent and original as Wodehouse's or Flann O'Brien's. It's always tempting to allow different criteria to apply to acting in musicals, to allow the artificiality of the medium to inform the performance. I wanted the actors to play truthfully, without sentimentality, to present a world larger than life without parody or facetiousness; to be true, in effect, to the 'fairy-tale'. Accents were studiously honed, the characters – even those on the periphery – were invested with offstage biographies. Runyon's stories were always on hand, and a professional croupier came in to teach us how to shoot craps.

We started rehearsals in early January – a seven-week stint, during which many of the cast had to learn from scratch to dance and sing harmonies, and all of them had to learn a tap routine. I was possessed by the idea that the show had to end with the entire cast tap-dancing down Broadway, and it was just as well that David Toguri was on hand to teach them. No choreographer I know has his skill and tact with actors, his invention and his indomitable good humour. And looking at the dancing of some of the cast at the early rehearsals, you'd have to say that he's an alchemist.

Guys and Dolls is essentially a play with music, the songs are always a logical extension of the dramatic situation and they always push the action forward, rather than allowing it to slow down or stand still. It's an irony that almost all the songs were written by Frank Loesser before the dialogue, which merely serves to highlight Loesser's genius as a dramatic lyricist. Abe Burrows wrote the book after an abortive script by Joe Swerling had been abandoned. 'Make it funny,' said George Kauffman, the director. 'But not *too* funny,' added Loesser. Abe Burrows certainly made it funny, but if I were looking for the catalytic talent that made *Guys and Dolls* so successful, I would lay six to five on Kauffman. He was a marvellous playwright (with Moss Hart and others – he was known as 'The Great Collaborator') and, as director, a *play-maker*, and he was an exacting and utterly professional craftsman. He insisted on regarding *Guys and Dolls* as a play interrupted by musical numbers. He felt this so strongly that he regarded most of the songs as 'lobby' numbers – every time a song started he sprinted for the lobby for a cigarette. Abe Burrows once overheard him, mid-sprint, mutter, 'Good God, do we have to do *every* number this son-of-a-bitch ever wrote?'

'This beats working,' said Bob Hoskins on more than one occasion. There were times when it didn't seem fair to be paid for having so much fun; in fact there were times when I would have happily paid to do what I was doing. We worked hard, but it wasn't hard work; the show is so well crafted that there is an almost mathematical precision to it that demands that you get it right. 'Musicals are not written, they're fixed,' runs the adage. If you're doing a show which has been fixed to perfection, run for countless performances in countless productions, you know that if something isn't working it's not the show's fault – it's yours. Ironically, this is comforting. For all this, there's nothing mechanical about the show; it has a life of its own and a heart as big as a skyscraper.

As the first night approached, everybody I met seemed to have seen the original Broadway production, or loved the film, knew every word of the lyrics, had played the parts or had married one of the chorus. If you do a major Shakespeare play you inherit the baggage of previous productions, and you are haunted by theatrical tradition. With *Guys and Dolls* I felt we were toying with something altogether more personal, and more passionate; a world of sentimental memories. The stakes were high, and gambling metaphors gushed in the press, like a burst watermain. What they said was true: we had to win this hand or crap out in ignominy. In the end, the joy that we took in the show was shared by the audience; we had a success. Critics, immobile as Lazarus, spoke of dancing down the South Bank; one of them, correctly, described the show as a 'love letter to Broadway'; and, thanks to David Toguri, I even learned to tap.

RICHARD III

Richard's occupation's gone. He's a successful soldier who, in the face of great odds, has welded a life together in which he has a purpose, an identity as a military man. His opening speech describes his depression at the conclusion of war, his bitterness at the effeminacy of peace. He is a man raging with unconsummated energy, needing a world to 'bustle' in. This hunger to fill the vacuum left by battle is the driving force of the play. It has a deep resonance for me. When I made the film about the Falklands War, I saw this sense of unfulfilled appetite at first hand in people who had fought in the war and were unable to come to terms with peace. The experience of battle is a profound distillation of fear, danger, and exhilaration; nothing in peacetime will ever match it, and those who are affected by it are as traumatised as those who have been wounded, who at least have the visible signs of trauma to show for it. Soldiers are licensed to break the ultimate taboo against killing; some of them get the habit.

Richard has had to fight against many odds; he is the youngest son, coming after two very strong, dominant, assertive, brothers – and he is deformed, 'unfinished'. His eldest brother, Edward, is a profligate, and the spectacle of his brother's success with women must be a sharp thorn in his flesh. The age (perhaps any age) worshipped physical prowess, and Richard is accustomed, though certainly not inured, to pejorative terms like 'bunch-back'd toad'; he has heard them all his life. We know that he is deformed, but the text repeatedly tells us he is a successful professional soldier. We have to reconcile the two demands of the text. Olivier's interpretation has become central to the mythology of the play, but the deformity that he depicts has never seemed to me plausibly compatible with what Shakespeare wrote. Ian McKellen plays Richard with a small hump, he has chronic alopecia, and he is paralysed down one side of his body. These three handicaps taken together are quite sufficient to account for all the abuse he attracts – but not too severe to stop him from serving as a professional soldier. Experience shows that even slight deformities are enough to inspire repulsion; modern reactions to disability haven't changed very much in this respect.

It is clear that Richard has been rejected from birth by his mother; she says so unequivocally to Clarence's children, and her words of contempt spoken to her son in front of his troops confirm this. It is impossible to escape the conclusion that Shakespeare is attempting to give some history, some causality, to Richard's evil.

The military ethos, and the alliance of personal motives with historical conditions are the common backgrounds of many twentieth-century tyrants. I started working on the production with Ian McKellen and Bob Crowley without any definite plan about the setting, but I felt we couldn't divorce it from our own era. The rise of a dictator and the accompanying political thuggery are the main topics of the play. We don't have to look far for analogies: our century has sophisticated and systematised tyranny beyond the dreams of the previous two millennia. We're spoilt for examples close to us. I had first-hand, if vicarious, knowledge of tyranny through strong personal ties of friendship in Romania, but we never sought to establish literal equivalents between medieval and modern tyrants.

The design of the production emerged empirically. We started with an empty model box, and put minimal elements into it – rows of overhead lamps to create a series of institutionalised public areas, a world of prisons and cabinet rooms and hospital corridors; places and areas of ceremonial display, set off against candlelit areas of private pain. We drew some parallels with the rise of Hitler, but these were forced by Hitler himself; his rise shadows that of Richard astonishingly closely, as Brecht showed in *Arturo Ui*. Specific elements of Hitler's ascent to power, or Mosley's to notoriety, were echoes that bounced off a timeless sounding board. The play is set in a mythological landscape, even if it draws on an apparently historically precise period; I say 'apparently' because Shakespeare treats historical incident with little reference to fact – incidents are conflated, characters meet whose paths never crossed, Tudor myths prevail.

Some critics see only Nazi imagery in the production. There is no Nazi imagery. There are specific references to our own English iconography: the cross of St George, the uniforms of the British army. When Richard comes to power he redesigns his uniforms and puts on an armband – as Shakespeare puts it: 'He is dressed in armour, marvellous ill-favoured.' The language of demagoguery in this century has a remarkable consistency; Stalin, Mao Tse-tung, Ceauşescu and Bokassa share a predilection for large banners, demonstrations, and military choreography. They all share the same architectural virus; totalitarianism consistently distorts proportion by eliminating human scale. Mass becomes the only consideration.

Although the production is set in the twentieth century, I wanted Richard to wear medieval costume in the coronation; it's like turning a telescope the wrong way round. Tyrants always invent their own ritual, synthetic ceremonies borrowed from previous generations in order to dignify the present and suggest an unbroken continuum with old traditions. Hitler played up all the themes of historical restitution. Napoleon, the little man from Corsica, designed the preposterous Byzantine ceremony which is represented in David's painting. Most of the English ritual, our so-called time-honoured ritual, is not very old either. The order of the last British Coronation, in 1953, had been almost wholly invented by Queen Victoria. For me, playing around with the period, like bringing on the armour at the end of the battle scene, was a way of showing in what sense medievalism and modern time co-exist; the past is consistently made to serve the needs of the present.

In the same way, superstitions and beliefs are used to manipulate individuals or crowds into submission. Tyrants commonly exploit astrology, prophecies or other extra-rational phenomena, or even subscribe to them themselves; reason is an enemy of absolute power. The non-rational needs no historical excuse. Of course, there are some medieval terrors which may have been finally exorcised and which have become meaningless to us. Standing as she does in a sterilised mortuary, a modern Lady Anne might be sceptical, if not grief-ridden, about a corpse's wounds bleeding afresh, but none of the characters, including Richard, can be totally fearless in the face of Margaret's curses. It is the residue of superstition, the awe of the supernatural, which makes the terror of her curses perfectly plausible, even to this day.

The female characters are as strong as in any of Shakespeare's plays. The legacy of men's cruelty is swept up by women who have been educated by the experience of grief. They have caused pain to Richard and they are taught by him to suffer: Elizabeth – proud, arrogant, and abusive of him, loses her brother and her sons; the Duchess of York – sealed in her own self-importance, openly contemptuous of her son, loses another son and grandchildren at his hands; Lady Anne – blinded by her grief and her hatred and seduced by him, loses her self-respect and, finally, her life. Only Queen Margaret needs no education at his hands. 'Teach me how to curse my enemies,' says Elizabeth to her. The three queens, who start from violently mutually opposed positions, are united by their common hatred of Richard and their suffering at his hands. Their models in our times are only too obvious: the women who wait in Chile and in Argentina for news of their sons who have 'disappeared', and the mothers I saw in Romania shortly after the Revolution, putting candles and flowers in the streets on the spots where their sons had been killed.

The part of Queen Margaret was cut from Olivier's film, and that of Elizabeth barely visible. Some recent productions leave out the incantatory scenes of sorrow. They are notoriously difficult to handle, and often found alien to modern sensibilities, but I think of them as the heart of the play. It is called The Tragedy of Richard III, and it is *their* tragedy that is being told.

Richard III is so much a one-man show in our acting tradition that the miseries visited on woman by the male appetite for power tend to be obscured, and with them the complex picture of English society transformed by tyranny. The crude villain of melodrama has managed to overrule a play of considerable political subtlety. Richard does not appear in an untainted Eden; his England is the world of *realpolitik*. Clarence and Edward have both committed crimes in the Civil Wars, Clarence even admitting his guilt to the Keeper; Queen Elizabeth's family are greedy parvenus; Buckingham, Stanley and Ely are all morally ambiguous. At the beginning of the play Clarence has just been capriciously arrested; such behaviour may be exceptional and outrageous, but not unprecedented. What right have any of the characters to call Richard a villain?

Hastings, the Prime Minister, is a politician's politician, expedient, and amoral – when he is told of the impending execution of his political enemies, he can't fault this transparent abuse of justice; within minutes he is himself under sentence of execution. 'The rest that love me, rise and follow me,' says Richard, and at this point self-preservation takes over from courage, morality, or political expediency. We all hope that we will never have to face such a choice in our lifetime. While we were working on this production, I discussed with Bob Crowley, who is Irish, what would happen should Britain become a fascist country. 'Well, I'd be in a concentration camp, for a start,' he said. 'OK,' I said. 'I run the National Theatre. At what point would I stand up and say "No"?' I wish I could have answered confidently,

'Immediately,' but I was mindful of Klaus Mann's *Mephisto* where an actor finds so many sound arguments to justify his co-operation with the Nazi regime. The erosion of liberties is always gradual, and it takes formidable courage to say 'No' when the consequence is imprisonment or worse. And where there is a crying need for reform, many might be tempted to agree that minor infringements of liberty are a small price to pay for the benefit of an able leader. The post-First World War German government of Hindenburg was so massively compromised that it made a strong case for those who thought it was high time some energetic man undertook to clean them out.

None of the characters in the play are ciphers, and they all have a very highly developed sense of class and status. They belong to a world of manipulative, upper-ranking officials, not a bourgeois world at all. The English aristocracy still exercises some power in this country – if only because our class system is kept in place by the existence of the Monarchy. As for their responsibility in the rise of tyranny, of course it's a matter of pure speculation. It's a metaphor, a way of saying that this could have happened, could happen here, even though I would like to believe that the British are inherently immune to fascism.

Tyranny creates a contagious climate of fear. Scenes like the arrest of the Scrivener at the end of his speech, confiding his fears to the audience, were suggested by what I'd seen in Eastern Europe – talking to friends who were visibly afraid, searching rooms for microphones, turning the TV on before speaking. When we see these symptoms of terror parodied in spy fiction, we forget how censorship of lives, feelings and speech effectively constricts the brain every hour of the day. The Scrivener, who tells us about the abuse of the judicial system prior to Hastings' execution, reminds us that to live in a tyranny is to be afraid even to think.

The play is a long journey into night, a journey studded with nightmares and references to dreams. All the characters realise their dreams of (mostly posthumous) retribution in Richard's nightmare: Richmond walks round in seraphic confidence and dances with Lady Anne; Edward's wife and children play happy families; Margaret is reinstated in her former splendour; Clarence, Rivers, Hastings and Buckingham taunt their executioner from the grave.

Richmond is a young man, almost a boy, in the hands of mature soldier-politicians who are promoting him. It is essential for their purposes that he succeed, and he is equally determined to show that he can succeed. The play ends with his triumph, but I wanted the final image to be an equivocal one, suggesting that the cycle of competing for power, and ensuing civil strife, could be repeated. Richmond's first entrance is set against a backdrop of a peaceful country village, in Devon, in fact, near where I was born, the England of 'summer fields and fruitful vines'. If I was asked what I thought Richmond was fighting for, it would be this idealised picture of England. To me it's more than a metaphor; it's a heartland.

POLITICS

A director needs to be somehow assertive and yet self-effacing, dogged and yet pliable, demanding yet supportive. If this sounds a prescription for a perfect marriage partner, then I suppose it is. Directors are ever hopeful of making a successful marriage of actor and character, text and design, play and audience, and, if they look hesitant, doubtful, and diffident, it is because they know just how difficult it is, as in real life, to make a marriage work.

Directors are not naturally public people, and are, mercifully, seldom obliged to endure the thumbscrew, rack and strappado of publicity that's an occupational liability for an actor. I was working with Maggie Smith when a biography of her came out. I asked her if she'd read it; she made a vinegary face. 'Good God, no,' she said. 'I couldn't. I'm an ostrich, I can't bear publicity.' I have more of the mole in me than the ostrich – emerging briefly into the light and then scuttling back with relief below the surface, but my job at the National Theatre has obliged me often to disguise myself as a politician, and strut around in the company of less retiring species.

Politicians live in a sort of hell, condemned to wear a public mask of optimism and decisiveness, and to mouth fictions as if they were objective truths. Doubt is banished; ambiguity prohibited. To concede fallibility is to admit weakness, and to agree with the opposition is to embrace folly. A politician will tell you as you stand on the deck of a sinking ship, with the water lapping your chin, that the vessel is still on course. Politicians do not talk; they

167

assert – 'The fact of the matter is . . .' – and since their faces are unmarked by the confusions and uncertainties that we all endure, it is small wonder that they enjoy so little public esteem. When people are asked what professions they admire, politicians always limp home last – well behind the journalists and the tax inspectors. John Updike says that 'celebrity eats the face' – and maybe the soul in the case of politicians.

I've had to become a politician of a sort, lobbying politicians, sponsors, even audiences. The pieces that follow are public utterances; their purpose was evangelical, and their voice is raised for the public platform, more booming than chatting.

MY COUNTRY RIGHT
OR WRONG

The *Sunday Telegraph* asked me to write this piece. I imagine that they had hoped for an 'I spit on the flag' piece judging by an interview with me that they had printed a month or two earlier. Conflating my left(ish) views with my admission that I found democracy in the theatre an entirely laudable principle but very hard to operate in practice, they came up with the headline: 'ENTER THE NATIONAL DICTATOR.' About the same time their sister newspaper the *Daily Telegraph* published a review of *Tumbledown* written by the Defence Correspondent on the grounds, I presume, that their TV critic couldn't be trusted to castigate with sufficient fervour and authority. They must have been disappointed with my failure to live down to expectations.

Until I was seventeen my feeling for the Country was almost exclusively derived from the country. I grew up in a landscape that seems to me now to define Englishness almost to the point of parody. It is the sort of landscape that sustained colonial exiles in a comfortable fiction of an unchanged and unchangeable homeland. Physically, in spite of some small-scale speculative building of stuccoed breeze-block bungalows, it still evokes the nineteenth century, socially an even earlier era. This is forelock-pulling country.

Situated at the epicentre of Englishness, my brain was willingly colonised by American culture – Marvel comics, rock-and-roll, movies and television: *I Love Lucy*, *The Burns and Allen Show*,

Bilko, and more. Like many of my generation in the late-fifties, I was a cultural Fifth Columnist for most of my formative years. I took the loveliness of the surrounding countryside for granted, and only fairly recently have I come to regret my indifference to the extraordinary privilege of growing up in a quite literally enchanted landscape – Arthurian as well as Hardy country – a landscape that, as a friend of mine says, makes you see the point of England.

I went to a public school dedicated more to social programming than to learning; its credo was Church, Queen, and Country. Like many of my contemporaries, I responded poorly to the propaganda. When I was thirteen we sat, formally, eighty of us, before our evening meal, and listened to Anthony Eden on the radio informing us that 'Colonel Nasser has naturalised, er, nationalised the Suez Canal. Britain must invade Egypt.' 'The honour of our country is at stake,' we were told by our housemaster. I was bemused. I was no less bemused twenty-six years later when I heard our Prime Minister say much the same thing about the Falkland Isles. As thirteen year olds we were not encouraged to ask questions, and it was left to a teenage wit to unearth Chesterton's *bon mot*: ' "My country right or wrong" is a thing that no patriot would think of saying except in a desperate case. It's like saying "My mother drunk or sober".'

I recoil still from appeals to 'country' and 'national culture', and in this I reveal my Englishness. We don't like to admit to nationhood or culture, or, especially, to ideology, although in some respects we are the most ideologically motivated nation in Europe. We used to be defined nationally by an empire, and now we are condemned to live out Dean Acheson's truism that 'Britain has lost an empire and has yet to find a role'. So we invent our roles on the domestic rather than the international stage. We put ourselves in inverted commas – 'Swinging London', 'The Rock Revolution', 'Punks', 'Fogeys', 'Sloanes', 'Beasties', 'Yuppies'. We put on funny accents; we make TV shows about TV shows; we make adverts based on old adverts; we have a whole culture that refers above all to itself. We have created a world fit for shop-fitting, in which presentation is paramount, and we excel in those media that put a premium on display: advertising and theatre.

For such a notoriously reticent and introspective nation we seem to have a great capacity for displaying ourselves in public. Maybe it's precisely because of this reticence that we like to express ourselves vicariously through the theatre, and that strain in our national character has given us what is unarguably the richest theatre tradition in the world. Whether it's the *best* must be left to those who keep statistics, write record books, and dream up a sport as daft as synchronised swimming.

There's an unparalleled wealth of plays that still bears reviving. If our theatres sometimes appear insular in their reluctance to scour the continental repertoire for plays unknown to British audiences, it's largely because we are spoilt for choice at home. We have a large range of talented actors, most of whom don't regard the theatre as a poor relation to film or TV and above all we have audiences with an appetite and curiosity, without which tradition becomes a ritual.

Our theatre reflects the strengths and weaknesses of our national character. It is almost wholly pragmatic, humane, often witty, often ironic, hardly ever didactic. The visual muscle is not well developed but is becoming more so, and is less often castigated nowadays for being insufficiently 'European'. This is a familiar criticism: for several hundred years critics have railed against the state of contemporary drama, and held up foreign drama and that of other ages as a stick with which to beat the present. Yet while audiences for other, more recent, forms of entertainment, such as football, dwindle, the theatre-going habit prevails. Its opponents are most frequently those who never go to the theatre and thus wish to deny the pleasure to those who do. They are those people who think, like C.S. Lewis, that life would be tolerable if it were not for its amusements.

Britain is gradually being converted into a theme park. Buildings, institutions, and ceremonies are appropriated, synthetically processed, and disgorged as 'national traditions'. If we really are to preserve traditions – if we really do value our heritage – then we should do everything we can to ensure continuity of the most animated and longest-lived part of that cultural heritage: our theatre.

Most of our commercial theatre is now fed directly or indirectly by subsidised theatre. *All* subsidised theatres are obliged to obey market forces in that their subsidy is much the smaller part of their revenue. Without consistently attracting audiences they would be bankrupt, and not just financially. The 'right to fail' is not a charter for self-indulgence, it's the necessary condition for all artistic enterprises, their equivalent of research and development. State subsidy and sponsorship provide the conditions for the continuity that is the lifeblood of our theatrical tradition.

The overwhelming irony of possessing this great theatrical tradition is that we've never fully accepted that it should be seen as an expression of our national identity and a matter of public pride. Our support for the arts has always been somewhat grudging and piecemeal. A commitment to supporting the arts (and for that matter the National Health Service and Education) to the same level as our European colleagues *would* make me proud of my country – right or wrong.

WHAT'S THE NATIONAL
THEATRE FOR?

I'm fairly sanguine about critics, even if I sometimes feel after a bad notice that the appropriate fate for the critic is what they did to the dead Pharaohs before embalming them – having their brains drawn out with a long hook. I'm consoled by Christopher Hampton's observation that we are bound to feel about critics as lampposts do about dogs, but I'm temperamentally unable to affect the detachment of Picasso, who recommended that artists regard critics as birds do ornithologists. I get hurt and I get irritated, but seldom more so than when I was taken to task by a critic for failing to provide a public manifesto for the National Theatre. I dislike manifestos of all sorts – with the exception of the Dadaist manifesto, which of course was Dadaist in that it is absurd to attempt to write a manifesto for any artistic enterprise. I believe, with George Devine, that as far as theatres go policy is who you work with, and I have got no nearer to a public statement of intent for the National Theatre than this piece which I wrote for the *Independent*.

In the Polish epic *The Knights of the Teutonic Order*, set in the early Middle Ages, a knight is tortured, his tongue is cut out, and he is imprisoned in an iron box for several years. He is eventually liberated from his confinement and he shambles out, grey-haired, sightless and tongueless, to rediscover a world whose features he can now only guess at. This is not light years away from my nightmares about the Château d'If on the South Bank. The reality is comfortingly different. The National Theatre is not an immutable bureaucracy, nor is it a cultural colossus riddled with institutional inertia. It is, to state what ought to be obvious, a theatre, or to be more obvious still, three theatres within one building, and people work in these theatres for the traditional reasons that are often loftily dismissed as being sentimental: a sense of community, 'family', a desire to share a common purpose.

The National Theatre exists to do work that, either by content or by execution or both, could not be performed or would not be initiated by the commercial sector. It provides continuity of 'investment', of employment, and of theatrical tradition, and this requires a subsidy to supplement the income from the box office. Recently an attempt has been made to blur the distinction between the commercial and the subsidised theatre in order to argue that there is no longer any real need for subsidy: if market forces can prevail for large nationalised businesses, so they should for large theatre companies. This conveniently ignores the fact that six nights a week, fifty-two weeks a year, the NT places 2,300 seats for sale in the 'market place', and depends for its survival on the sale of at least 1,750 of them.

No doubt the subsidised theatres have conspired in undermining their status by presenting shows that appear to be governed by a commercial imperative indistinguishable from the West End, and the relentless emphasis on productivity, cost-effectiveness, mixed economies, and profit margins has obscured the real issue which is not about money but art – sorry, the three-letter word just slipped out. The case for the existence of subsidised theatres is made on their stages and the only questions worth asking are, 'Is what I see on the stage any good?' and, 'What does it mean to me?'

The policy of the National Theatre has been diverse and pluralistic and will remain so. At heart I'm a populist, but I don't mean by this that all standards are reduced to the common denominator of 'popular' culture, where the only criterion of success is measured in numbers; I mean that art can and should be popular and accessible even if its content is complex and disturbing. A theatre without an audience doesn't amount to a hill of beans, but that fact shouldn't license the NT to act as a quasi-commercial production house. The commercial theatre is defined by its need to make a profit; the subsidised theatre is defined by its need to be good.

Any organisation that has the word 'National' attached to it (let alone 'Royal') must be expected to fulfil some sort of exemplary function, and a theatre's activities are rather more conspicuous than a hospital or sports centre. I worked for many years in theatres outside London and looked, with a mixture of envy, irony, and longing, at the large metropolitan 'centres of excellence'. When I became the NT's director I was acutely conscious of the obligation for the theatre to live up to its name: the title of The National Theatre of Great Britain and Northern Ireland can be viewed with some cynicism if its work is constantly confined to the concrete casing of its building on the South Bank. It's imperative that the NT tours extensively on a small and large scale, nationally and internationally, and that we form significant links with regional theatres through co-production and exchanges; we should replace the upper case of '*N*ational' with the lower case of '*n*ational'.

Composing the content of the repertoire will always be a balancing act between adventure and caution, between known classics and the unknown, recent plays and new ones, but the spine of the work will always be the classics. They are our genetic link with the past and our means of decoding the present. Every age sees its own reflection in these plays. We find in them not the past throwing a shadow on the present, but a distorted image of ourselves – our questions, our doubts and confusions. The classics survive not because they are relics venerated for their age but because of what they mean to us *now*. This is not a specious assertion of their 'relevance' or social usefulness; these are the twin mantras of a style of production in which the play's meanings are pounded into a small mass in order to conform to an epigrammatic concept; the result inevitably supports the Goldwynism 'Let's have some new clichés'.

We have to keep rediscovering ways of doing the classics. They don't have absolute meanings. There is no fixed, frozen, way of doing them. Nobody has mined a play and discovered a definitive way of doing it, and to pretend that there are fixed canons of style, fashion, and taste is to ignore history. Nostalgia is a powerful, if slow-acting toxin, and it can cripple; the life of a theatre should always be in the present tense.

The larger part of our classical repertoire is the collection of plays written between 1580 and 1640. It takes only a mildly literate theatre-goer to name at least ten indisputably great plays of that era. Almost all these plays are in verse, and there's the rub. Any attempt to come to terms with them must confront their form; the life of the plays is in the language, not alongside it, or underneath it. Feelings and thoughts are released at the moment of speech. An Elizabethan audience would have responded to the pulse, the rhythms, the shapes, sounds, and above all meanings, within the consistent ten-syllable, five-stress, lines of blank verse. They were an audience who *listened*.

Verse drama places demands on the audience, but a greater demand still on the actors, habituated by naturalistic speech, and to private, introspective, emotional displays. In dramatic poetry the appeal is all to the physical and emotional resources. As Eliot said:

There is a fringe of indefinite extent, or feeling, which we can only detect, so to speak, out of the corner of the eye and can never completely focus; of feeling of which we are only aware in a kind of temporary detachment from action . . . This peculiar range of sensibility can be expressed by dramatic poetry, at its moments of greatest intensity. At such moments, we touch the border of those feelings which music can only express.

It should be the principal aim of a National Theatre to make the theatre expressive in the way that Eliot describes: to do justice to the verbal *and* the visual imagery. In short, to make the theatre as expressive and singular a medium as possible. It's impossible to overestimate the difficulties, and a wholly successful theatre performance is about as rare as a dry day in June; when seen, it is, as Coleridge said of Kean, 'like reading Shakespeare by flashes of lightning'. We should aspire to make every theatre performance, of plays ancient and modern, as vivid, and as unforgettable. I hope there will be many such experiences at the National Theatre over the next few years, but wilful optimism alone is worthless; it's only the end result that matters.

I am haunted by Voltaire's observations about the theatre in *Candide*:

'How many plays have been written in French?' asked Candide.

'About five or six thousand,' replied the Abbé.

'That's a lot,' Candide remarked. 'How many are any good?'

'Fifteen or sixteen,' replied the other.

'That's a lot,' said Martin.

WHAT ARE THE ARTS FOR?

On a damp day in autumn 1989 I was invited to attend a meeting at the Queen Elizabeth Hall. It was in honour of National Arts Advocacy Day and was organised by the National Campaign for the Arts, a monument to the years when state funding for the arts was under a real threat from a government determined to lobotomise the 'welfare state mentality'.

Government opposition to the arts had the effect of politicising a group of people who had, up till then, been a disunited diaspora. Musicians stood beside actors, painters beside film-makers, to listen to a series of passionate and bellicose speeches. Like those grainy films of CND marches, it would probably seem quaintly futile and self-regarding now, but at the time there was a thrilling sense of standing together to make a common chorus.

It may have done some good. Three years later, we were being drenched in election promises like showers of acid rain, but at least one of these promises came good: a minister was appointed for the arts with cabinet status, and the prospect of treasure trove in the shape of a National Lottery.

I hope I'm not alone in finding that the idea of a national Arts Advocacy Day comes as something of a surprise. It's a surprise that the arts *need* advocacy. Like most of us here today I grew up in a world where the arts, like the Roman Conquest in *1066 and All That*, were unquestionably a 'Good Thing'. To be for the arts was to be as uncontroversial as the preacher who was heard by Calvin Coolidge preaching against sin. What had the preacher said about sin, Coolidge was asked. 'He was against it,' said the President.

We're living in an age where we've lost faith in what's worth being for or against, in what it's worth preserving or destroying. The certainties of the few infect the rest of us with uncertainty and doubt; instead of celebrating the arts on their own terms, we seek to justify them on the specious grounds of cost-effectiveness, or as tourist attractions, or as investments, or as commodities that can be marketed, exploited and profited from.

The arts make their own argument. They are part of our life, our language, our way of seeing, the measure of our civilisation. I can understand politicians resenting poets being described as the unacknowledged legislators of the world, but I find it hard to understand carrying that resentment to an active discouragement of poetry throughout the educational system. It's not just that the arts tell us truths about ourselves and our feelings and our society that reach parts of us that politics and journalism don't. The arts, above all, help us to make sense of the world; they help us to fit the disparate pieces together; to try and make form out of chaos. Beyond this, or even *before* this, they entertain, they give pleasure, they give hope, they ravish the senses.

In fact, in many ways, art is all the things that politics isn't. It's not polemic; it's not ideology. The best art, by definition, is passionate, ambiguous, complex, mysterious, thrilling – all qualities that we seek in art because they exist in our private lives even if they don't in our public ones.

My own particular territory, the subsidised theatre, now seems to be as much under threat as the Amazonian rain forest, and there are as sound reasons for preserving the one as the other. We have in this country a *living* theatre tradition that is literally the envy of the world.

The subsidised theatre acts as a source of artistic capital (if we must use the language of the money market) for the whole of theatre, television, and film in this country. All the skills of actors, directors, writers, designers, and technicians are to be found not only in the grandiosely named 'centres of excellence' – the national companies – but in repertory theatres up and down the country, fringe theatre, and touring companies, large and small arts centres, theatre-in-education groups, children's theatre companies, and community theatres. The Royal Court Theatre in Sloane Square, the Theatre Royal in Stratford East, and the Royal National Theatre on the South Bank share much more than a Royal title. They belong to a common body – if we chop off limbs to allow them to atrophy, we damage not just the extremities but the health of the whole.

I think today's agenda begs the question of why the arts should be supported by the government if they can't survive in the open market. I can't, or won't, get drawn into detail about the building costs and labour costs that are inherent in the presentation of live theatre. Or indeed what seems to me self-evidently different about what we do to what the commercial theatre does. I will say this: the spectre of market forces has been constantly invoked to frighten we feckless children in the arts world. The theatre in this country goes back four hundred years and understood market forces before the word monetarism had even been coined. All subsidised theatres depend on the market, respond to the market, and wither if they fail to achieve their box-office targets. No theatre in this country is given a charter to play to empty houses, or even to half-full houses. In my own theatre we are obliged to achieve a capacity throughout the year which would send a commercial management running to the sedative if not the sanatorium.

We don't, moreover, need to be lectured about marketing and good business practice. The sandwich board, the handbill, the billboard, were *invented* by theatre managements long before the advertising industry received its contemporary canonisation. And at least in my limited experience of business – largely confined to encounters with the building and garage trade – the theatre is the *only* business that delivers its goods exactly on time, and at the advertised price.

That we need government money and business sponsorship should not be regarded as a sign of weakness, but rather a sign of confidence in our own culture and society. If what we are really talking about is political persuasion, let me make a simple point: at the moment the parties are risking life and limb in their eagerness to out-Green their opponents. Two years ago it was an inviolable political truth that there were no votes in Green issues. Let no party imagine that the same could not be true of the arts. Man cannot live by bread alone; or as Napoleon said: 'When people cease to complain, they cease to think.'

Let's complain as loudly as we can. We need the arts in order to think. And we need to think in order to survive.

BONFIRES ON THE MOON:
THEATRE OF THE NINETIES

Paul Hamlyn, the publisher, is a creature as rare as the coelacanth; he is a socialist millionaire. He gave money to the Labour Party to develop a strategy for the arts, and, as a way of encouraging debate, their Shadow Minister invited a number of people in the arts to deliver lectures in the Grand Committee Room at the Houses of Parliament.

My lecture was delivered on a baking hot day in July in 1991, and beforehand, nearly catatonic with performer's nerves, I gained solace from pacing the flagstones outside the Committee Room, in the great gothic expanse of Westminster Hall. Here King Charles had been sentenced to death, Churchill had lain in state, and it seemed almost bathetic to wander in its cool darkness anticipating the scrutiny of a number of Members of Parliament. As it turned out, there was a fullish house but a conspicuous absence of MPs of any party. The most celebrated figure in the audience was a frail, almost elfin, old man, who sat near the front, and smiled sweetly and encouragingly whenever I caught his eye. Sometimes he dozed, but I thought the weather might be partly to blame. I met him afterwards; he thanked me for being so optimistic and said his name was Yehudi Menuhin. I was very touched.

A little time ago I was, as Bertie Wooster would say, pronging the moody yolk, when I read an article which began with the words: 'The theatre is finished.' I prepared myself for the worst. It was written by no less an authority than Quentin Crisp, who lives in New York and by his own admission has not been to the theatre to see a play for years if he can help it. Similar unprompted obituaries had been pronounced over the previous few months. Theatre had been described as 'a spoiled brat', 'a relatively minor art', 'impoverished in imagination', 'hopeless', 'dull', 'feeble', 'scelerotic', 'rotten', and just plain 'bad'. Not all of this has been written by Bernard Levin, even if he had, like a zealous priest, pronounced that out of 15,000 plays in the last twenty years only forty were any good.

Levin has provided the culture for this anti-theatre virus to breed. Other columnists have sprayed us intermittently with their views on the theatre. I can only hope that they aren't contagious, or that we're robust enough to withstand them. As a consolation at least we have the manifest glories of British journalism.

It's an affectation of journalists to pretend that they're detached from the things that they're writing about. I can't pretend that I'm capable of such objectivity. I like the theatre. I like going to the theatre. I like the medium of theatre. I like its buildings. Well, most of them. And I like the people who work in them. Most of them. It is true that I have a vested interest, and it's also true that I can't help feeling a sort of ironic bemusement at the thought that I have presided over a dead theatre which has just enjoyed its best year ever at the box office.

I came to the theatre, like most things in my life, comparatively late. I started going to the theatre seriously when I was eighteen, in the early-sixties. The start of my theatre-going coincided with a period of extraordinary optimism. It's natural enough, perhaps, that theatrical energy and invention coincide with periods of economic expansion: the Elizabethan and Jacobean ages, the Restoration, the late-eighteenth century, the late-nineteenth century, the mid-fifties, sixties and seventies in this century. I was able to see the work of Joan Littlewood at Stratford East, the Royal Court in its most fertile years, the newly formed RSC under Peter Hall, and the newly formed National Theatre at the Old Vic. *Oh What a Lovely War, The Wars of the Roses,* Brook's *Lear*, Olivier's

Othello; the young Maggie Smith, the young Albert Finney, the young Vanessa Redgrave; the plays of Arnold Wesker, of Harold Pinter, John Osborne, Peter Shaffer, Peter Nichols, Edward Bond, David Storey, Charles Wood, Tom Stoppard; Scofield, Richardson, Gielgud, Guinness, Peggy Ashcroft, even Edith Evans, and Kenneth Tynan presiding over this activity as a mandarin and godfather. It seemed to me that anything and everything was possible.

What I liked about the theatre, and what I continue to like, is precisely what some people hate about it. I like the fallibility that goes hand in hand with the immediacy. It happens in the present tense. It's vulnerable, changeable, maddeningly so sometimes. I like the sense of occasion, the event, the participation in what I'll unrepentantly describe as a communal act. There are those for whom these words smack of religion, tambourines and evangelism; there are those for whom it smacks of the devotions of local government, coffee cups and committees; and there are those, I suppose, for whom it smacks of group sex. But for me it smacks of the theatre, magic and moral debate.

There are many good reasons for *not* going to the theatre. I once spoke to the financier James Goldsmith in the hope of luring him into sponsoring a play at the National Theatre. 'I never go to the theatre,' he said. 'My legs are too long.' And I have a friend, a film director, who hates going to the theatre because it's all in wide shot. Many people prefer the cinema for its solitary, dreamlike disengagement. John Updike, a writer for whom I have a great admiration, said:

> I've never much enjoyed going to plays. The unreality of painted people standing on a platform saying things they've said to each other for months is more than I can overlook.

For me this is missing the point. It is the recreation that animates the art and makes it unique. All art forms are unreal in some sense. They have their formal rules, their conventions, their partiality, novels as much as paintings. Most of us unconsciously avoid the error of the woman who said to Matisse: 'Surely the arm of this woman is too long?' To which Matisse replied, 'It's not an arm, madam, it's a picture.'

Each art form has its unique properties. There is no art that uses time, space, gesture, movement, speech, colour, costume, light and music in the way that the theatre does. It thrives on metaphor; things stand *for* things rather than being the thing itself, a room can become a world, a group of characters a whole society. It invokes the astonishment of the unreal, the strange, magnified proportions that occur naturally in childhood.

The theatre is an activity where the event itself, the performance, is influenced by the audience; without the audience a performance is as meaningless as a bicycle without wheels. The audience has to obey certain social rules. It has to consent to the participation, which at the very least means sitting in the dark without talking for longish periods. There are many people I know who find this an unconscionable restriction of their freedom and feel compelled to supplement the dialogue with their own commentary. Judi Dench told me of a woman who had sat through a performance of *The Three Sisters* embroidering the play throughout with her seamless monologue. As the final moments approached and the three tear-stained heroines clung to each other she achieved immortality as she muttered to her friend, 'You know, I think they're sisters.'

The theatre is as variable in quality as any art; when it's bad it's as dismal and redundant a social ritual as Beating the Bounds of the City of London. It can be inert, dispiriting, clubby, self-regarding, and embarrassing. To be part of an audience on such an occasion can make one ashamed to be part of the human race, let alone the same profession as the people on the stage. In my insufficiently brief career as an actor I played in many such productions.

It's a virtue of the theatre that it's hard to be indifferent to it when it's bad. A bad film can be shrugged off with a bag of popcorn, or even finding the exit. To leave a theatre performance is to make a public gesture of criticism. It is precisely that danger of an audience exercising its right to vote with its feet that makes the theatre, at least potentially, such an alluring and dangerous medium.

The British are said to have the finest theatre in the world. Since we are told the same thing about our television, our judiciary, and our parliamentary system, we can perhaps be forgiven for being a little sceptical of this claim. We have, certainly, very high expectations of our theatre and are consequently disappointed if it fails to live up to them. We inherit the traditions of Shakespeare, Marlowe, Jonson, Webster, Middleton; of Farquhar and Congreve; of Wilde, of Shaw, of O'Casey (all Irish, of course); of D. H. Lawrence, of Harold Brighouse, of Coward, Rattigan, and so on. And so on. Not to mention the litany of names of great actors, actor-managers and directors. The British theatre has laid its palm print on every country where theatre exists, with the possible, and characteristic, exception of France. Our theatre has inspired Pushkin and Goethe, Chekhov and Schiller, Ibsen, Eugene O'Neill, David Mamet, Stanislavski and Brecht. A collaborator told Brecht of an English play called *The Beggar's Opera* that combined music, speech, and moral satire. 'Ah,' said Brecht. 'That smells of theatre.'

The British have an enthusiasm for theatre because so many of the characteristics of the medium coincide with the characteristics of the nation. The theatre exploits ritual, processions, ceremonies, heiratic behaviour and dressing up. It depends on adversarial conflict, the stuff of our parliamentary and legal system. It is concerned with role-playing, second nature to a nation obsessed with the signs and manners of class distinction, and inured to the necessity, as a nation and as individuals, of pretending to be what you aren't.

Perhaps this is the reason we produce such an extraordinary richness of acting talent. I don't think it's foolish or vainglorious to say that we do have the best actors in the world. There are a remarkable number who are not only gifted but resourceful, pragmatic, witty, humane, generous, irreverent and courageous.

In some respects they're like soldiers, veterans of many ill-conceived campaigns, always ready to commit themselves to action, but ever-sceptical of the leaders who have dragged them there. I don't think it is a coincidence that Shakespeare was not only an actor but spent his time in the company of actors. They can be as vain, difficult, petty and selfish as any group of lawyers, politicians, journalists or chefs, but I would rather spend my time with a group of good actors than with any other professional body.

The National Theatre recently took two Shakespeare productions on a tour of Europe. In Hamburg the productions were held up to the German theatre (a nice irony here) as prime examples of 'poor' theatre, productions that used, to German eyes, minimal resources and placed their trust wholly on the heads of the actors. The characteristic which, above all, makes British actors interesting is the very quality which threatens the continuing existence of their world: their pragmatism, their genius for adapting to all conditions whatever resources are available. Two planks and a passion; what's the show and where's the stage?

While we readily celebrate the vitality of our theatre traditions we are reluctant to do enough to guarantee their survival. To do so requires a greater intervention from the state and an attitude that is anything but pragmatic. It is one of the more appealing characteristics of our nation that we have a well-developed suspicion of dogma and ideology. The corollary of that, however, is that we refuse to concede that in some respects our ideological convictions are all the stronger for being unexamined. The belief in the Monarchy, the House of Lords, the Honours system, and the 'British Way of Life' is as powerful and passionate as any religious dogma or political credo and is all the more resilient for not appearing as such.

Likewise we do not speak as do the French or Germans or Italians of our 'culture' and apply political forces to engendering or embellishing it. We invent a curious but admirable conceit called the Arts Council in order to 'develop and improve the knowledge, understanding and practice of the arts', to quote its original Charter.

The cry goes up: what is so special about art that it requires these tender ministrations? Isn't it all ballet dancers in pink tights, and fat men with loud voices asking to be feather-bedded by the state to indulge elitist hobbies? Why should the arts be protected where popular culture is not? These are not easy questions to answer; the reply that the arts are special because they are *special* is, somehow, rather lame and unsatifying. So we mumble such truisms as 'the pursuit of excellence', 'the pursuit of meaning', 'trying to make sense of the world', 'testifying to its chaos', 'comforting with its beauty'. It is, we say, the voice of God speaking through Man, mitigating our pain and elevating our hope. Or maybe we should just say that art is life with the dull bits left out. Whatever you say there is nothing that can convert the confirmed philistines but art itself, and they are already inoculated against that.

The sophisticated philistine will argue that art is *too* special to be left to the state and that it must *ipso facto* be deregulated. I recognise this argument as the same made by the *Daily Telegraph* Defence Correspondent commenting to a friend of mine when *Tumbledown* was shown: 'I'm all for knocking the Establishment. I am choosy about who does it.'

Some supporters of subsidy for the arts on the Right will advocate subsidy on the grounds of their cost-effectiveness, or their use as a tourist enticement, or as a visible or invisible export; even, sometimes, on the grounds that there is a good return on the original investment in VAT, tax and savings on unemployment benefit.

From the Left we hear of their social usefulness, rather as a nineteenth-century curate's wife might advocate distributing informative pamphlets to the deserving poor. In addition they seek, sometimes, to take away from art the very thing that makes it alluring: its mystery. A recent motion to the 'Arts for Labour' AGM advocated the need to 'take the mystery . . . out of the word *art*', pointing out that opera, theatre, variety, TV and popular music fall under the same category. By all means let's make art as accessible, both physically and intellectually, as variety, TV or popular music, but don't rob it of its chance to enchant; don't, as an Eastern European dissident said, 'exchange the wizard's robe for the coat of the social engineer'.

This is a view of art that treats past art merely as a preparation for future art, whose mission can be summed up in a single phrase: to educate. It denies fantasy the chance to be commonplace, and reality the chance to be mysterious. Instead of taking pleasure in the arts as a private affair they are held up solely as a means of social insight.

Politicians are wary of art because it is wayward and ambiguous, because it deals with unquantifiable feelings rather than facts. Lenin confessed that he was afraid to listen to Beethoven because when he did he felt like caressing people's heads when it was necessary to beat them. Most politicians in this country are more interested in having their own heads caressed and respond in wounded bewilderment when they discover that the arts that they have allowed to flourish through their patronage wish to retain the right to criticise and to mock them. It is irritating to have to endure the often noisy dissent of an apparently arrogant and self-interested clique but it has always been hard for rulers to license the jester as well as the judge.

There is another and more insidious argument against subsidy. The dictates of artistic endeavour are very harsh and its creatures are governed by the law of survival of the fittest. Talent, vision and will-power are the currency of this world and they regulate its fortunes as ruthlessly as any market economy. It is tempting, therefore, to think that the funding of the arts should be made to float on the same principle. In the case of the performing arts this is simply incompatible with survival. The performance of a symphony requires upwards of a hundred people, an opera sometimes twice that number. It may be cost-effective to leave out the double basses in a performance of a Beethoven symphony, but it will be music only to the accountant's ears. And whatever arguments may be made by small theatre companies desperate for survival, a Shakespeare play cannot be properly performed with less than fifteen actors.

If we want a national theatre, and by this I mean a theatre in the nation and not merely one that resides in a concrete shell on the South Bank, we must be prepared to recognise that by *definition* it cannot function without subsidy. Of course it is possible to make a profit out of running individual shows for as long as there is an audience and investors, but if we want a theatre that takes artistic risks, sustains the best of tradition, develops new talent, underwrites the commercial theatre, and does all this at seat prices that do not exclude all but the very rich, then we must seek state support. To pretend otherwise is either wilfully destructive, or it's like lighting bonfires on the moon, pointless and self-extinguishing.

There's a peculiarly obnoxious phrase that is used to describe the public's reluctance to continue to support the multitude of pleas from charitable organisations; it's called 'compassion fatigue'. I'm sure there's an equivalent term used to describe the weariness and encroaching deafness that is engendered by listening to those in the theatre recite their catechism of misery. And we've become prisoners of our own propaganda: we brandish our success and our indispensability while at the same time lamenting our decline and our poverty. This is confusing for a public that has enough trouble at the best of times understanding the nature of public subsidy.

When my production of *Guys and Dolls* was playing at the National Theatre I was deluged with requests from friends for tickets. Flattered as I was by their interest, I was bemused at how often I was expected to pay for them on the grounds that since the show was a success I must be doing well out of it. In vain I explained that subsidised theatres are fuelled by objectives other than profit for their employees. In the light of which, what are we to make of a poll taken in 1986 when British Telecom was privatised which showed that people felt that it was more accessible, worked more to their benefit, and was more democratic as a private company than as a state one? We're confronted here by a formidably deep-seated, and no doubt well-earned, fear of state control.

It's a fear that has enough substance to take seriously. Can we be sure that we haven't created an artificial culture where there isn't a spontaneous demand but one where the relationship between artists and audience has been engineered and is based on 'obligation' rather than on free will? The manifestation of this is the existence of paintings that have no *raison d'être* but to hang on the walls of large contemporary art galleries, or plays that have no purpose but to flesh out the repertoires of our large public theatres. In short, wherever there is state support for the arts there is danger of hardening of the arteries, of the growth of a museum culture.

We have to accept this danger as an occupational hazard; that there are sometimes bad plays and lifeless productions in our subsidised theatres is, in itself, no argument against subsidy. Nor is it true that the success of the good plays in our subsidised theatres is in some way less authentic than the success of plays which have flourished on Shaftesbury Avenue. Any commercial manager would have envied the success of *Amadeus* and *Pravda* but would have been both unwilling and unable to take the risk of producing them in the first place. A mutual dependency exists now between the commercial and the subsidised theatre; starve the one and you stifle the other.

We don't need to look far in the theatre to see the consequences of the gradual erosion of subsidy, accompanied, like a pilgrim's rather than a rake's progress, by the Sapping of Morale, and the Starving of Invention. In the seventies I worked mostly in the regional theatre. When I became Director of Nottingham Playhouse in 1973 I was lucky enough to work with several of a new generation of playwrights who were young, ambitious, cocky and keen to repudiate the old avant-garde and establish a new one. They embraced new forms, new kinds of staging, vivid use of language, of music, of design. There was a new awareness of the place of women in theatre (and outside it), a new assertiveness about the place of ethnic minorities, a new directness about political issues. New theatres were opened, often small, poky, and unprepossessing, but theatres nevertheless. New audiences followed. The mood was ebullient. Bliss it was to be alive.

This spontaneous explosion was underwritten by an Arts Council which was able, financially and philosophically, to play the role of the unappreciated protector of the ungrateful young. The Arts Council also fostered an initiative to devolve theatrical power from London to the regions. How familiar this sounds. This was an ambitious and far-sighted scheme whose intention was to establish six regional 'national' theatres in, if I remember rightly, Bristol, Nottingham, Birmingham, Manchester, Liverpool and Newcastle.

The failure to achieve this can of course be fairly ascribed to shortage of money, but it was also failure of will: the Arts Council didn't want it enough, and the theatrical profession was too supine, and *too* pragmatic. In addition, the drain of resources towards the centre was too compelling. The National Theatre had just moved to the South Bank and I was one of a number of directors of small London and regional theatres who signed a letter that expressed our concern that the apparently all too finite resources for the regions would be eaten up by the centre. It is a touching commentary on the ethos of the period that we sent our letter to *The Times*.

With hindsight our opportunistic self-concern turned out to be wisdom. The RSC expanded to mimic the new National Theatre, the initiative to devolve resources to the regions vapourised, and a generation of directors stayed at the two large national companies without ever running regional theatres. A new ethos emerged: younger directors seemed to lack the interest of the previous genera- tion in nursing new writing, in running companies and in nurturing new acting talent. A haphazard empirical process was lost, and lost too was the unspoken sense of shared experience between theatres in Newcastle, Nottingham, Exeter, and London.

The atomisation of regional theatre was assisted by what we came to misname Thatcherism. The theatre, as much as any other area of life, became infected by the virus of opportunism. A kind of impatience grew. Actors who might previously have been content to do a year or two in a regional theatre looked anxiously for parts on TV, in films, or the national companies. Casting directors proliferated, talent brokers spotting actors at drama schools, prematurely promoting their talents and adding to their impatience with the previous *de facto* forms of apprenticeship.

Impatience was accompanied by voraciousness. New talent, actors, writers, directors, was greedily pursued by the national companies whose allure and purchasing power was greater than the regional companies. In their turn the national companies were frequently outbid by TV and by the revived film industry in its brief, but cloudy, summer.

The ecology (and the economy) of the theatre started to resemble more and more the nation as a whole. We were in the age of the entrepreneur. 'Enterprise' was the mantra of the times, chanted with an incantatory fervour which suggested that its propagators felt that it could only be achieved by sympathetic magic.

The arts as a whole started to look fragile and none more so than the theatre, whose concern with moral issues started to look quaint when set against an obsession with graphic style, fashion photography and Ford Cortinas. In a sense the theatre will *always* be unfashionable because of its form, its need for order in narrative and in structure. It will always lag behind a society that is conspicuous for its formlessness, and its concern with the frailty of being human will always look defenceless when set against *Mad Max III* and *The Exterminator*, or the confident certainties of politics and journalism.

This growing vulnerability has been underscored by the gradual accession of the Arts Council to the prevailing ethos. It has become an apologist, a participant in the 'culture of enterprise' rather than in the enterprise of culture. An organisation that is responsible for the distribution of funds is bound to have its destiny shaped by the quantity of funds allocated to it and the respect accorded to it by the government of the day. The decline of both funds and respect has sapped its will and encouraged it to dabble in the shallows of social engineering, sponsorship, and marketing initiatives; the business of business rather than the business of art. The proliferation of planning initiatives, incentives, scrutinies, and strategies can't help but make one think that, like a dog barking in a large field, it is being done to remind us that it is there.

The arts world can't help being suspicious of these activities. The much-trumpeted strategies of the last few years – *The Glory of the Garden* and *The Cork Report* on the theatre – have sunk without trace. I don't think they were commissioned in bad faith, but from this perspective it looks as if the only real strategy was that of temporarily silencing dissent. A strategy without funds to implement it is like a smartly packaged children's game; you open it to find immensely detailed and complex instructions. The aim of the game, say the instructions, is to rearrange the enclosed pieces into different patterns. It will give hours of fun. The cruel disappointment is the discovery that the finite number of pieces can only be arranged in a finite number of shapes. We were naive to have taken the game more seriously than it was intended, and perhaps the best epilogue of *The Glory of the Garden* would be that provided by Noël Coward:

> Begging Kipling's pardon
> Of one thing I am sure
> That if England is a garden
> You're sure to find manure.

It's too easy to be unfair on the Arts Council, but it's hard not to find some comedy in the spectacle of a hundred per cent state-supported organisation giving advice on marketing to people who have no option but to attract an audience in order to survive. 'We who live to please must please to live,' as Molière said, and there was little *he* didn't know about patronage by the state. The new pluralism changes nothing; we lose our audience, we lose our jobs.

The Arts Council has a twin brief: to support excellence and to give access to the arts. It is underfunded in its twin role and is therefore bound to come unstuck. An eighteenth-century social reformer called Charles Fournier imagined a utopia in which the sea would lose its salt and taste like lemonade, and the world would blossom with 37 million playwrights all as good as Molière. The Arts Council hasn't quite as ambitious a strategy for utopia but its attempts to come close to it by its quasi-political initiatives for education and training, broadcasting, ethnic minorities, the disabled, all thoroughly worthwhile in themselves, have led merely to great frustration through lack of new money to implement the plans. Add to this the strain of pursuing policies for the regions, which are implicitly in direct contradiction of the government's, and the inability to make discretionary judgements because the organisations being judged have the (often legitimate) excuse that they can't improve the work while they are underfunded, and it is not hard to see that paralysis will ensue. Given this diagnosis it is a wonder that the patient is mobile at all.

I wish the remedy weren't so apparently crude and yet so manifestly complicated. Things can only get better with the application of more money, but money alone never produced any art worth having. 'Artists,' said Gorky, 'can't be forced like rhubarb.' One can't legislate for talent; it is inequitable, unpredictable and finite. If God plays dice with the world nowhere is it more apparent than in the distribution of talent, and all that money can do to help is allow it to breathe, be educated, be trained, be exercised, be recognised and be enjoyed.

There are two questions begged by the advocacy of this remedy: (1) How much money should the arts have? (2) Who will distribute it and to whom?

A recession is not the best time to be bidding for funds for the arts, and set against the claims of health, social services and education the arts can only end up looking like Oliver Twist. It's impossible to make any recommendations about arts funding without straying into politics but it's also an affectation to pretend the arts and politics *aren't* interconnected. We should take seriously what Auden said about art and politics:

> In our age, the mere making of a work of art is itself a political act. So long as artists exist, making what they please and think they ought to make, even if it's not terribly good, even if it only appeals to a handful of people, they remind the management of something managers need to be reminded of, namely, that the managed are people with faces, not anonymous numbers, that *Homo Laborens* is also *Homo Ludens*.

I believe that, if for no other reason than self-interest, the government should aim to spend a total of twelve per cent of the public spending budget on education instead of the seven per cent currently spent, with a commitment to increase arts spending within that allocation by a huge, exponential, transforming amount; a leap for education *and* the arts from insecurity to stability. This increase in spending on education and the arts would merely bring us into line with France and Germany. If we are to look at our rivals in the European Community it's at least thought-provoking to find ourselves at the top of the league in defence expenditure, and second from the bottom in public spending on culture, lagging well behind Italy, Greece and Portugal.

There are large numbers of schoolchildren who have been disenfranchised by our educational system from either practising or enjoying the arts. If talent is lucky enough to be recognised in schools, in the face of an ever increasing absence of music and drama teaching, there is virtually no grant aid available for training. It is one thing to invite talented young actors to get on their bikes to go to drama schools; it's quite another thing to demand it of people who can't afford a bike, let alone their accommodation.

Nor is there money available for theatre visits. The current educational curriculum, as devised by Mr Gradgrind, regards such things as frivolously inessential, with the result that more children are alienated from the arts, the arts become even more the exclusive territory of the middle class, and the more difficult it becomes in the future to justify their public support. It is not too late to reverse the spiral. The arts should be available as an educational facility as much as schoolbooks and sporting facilities. If you educate an audience you generate a new one, and one which may remain for life.

In return for the investment, the government must insist that artists have a democratic obligation to create structures which make sure that their work is available to as wide a constituency as possible. To advocate, as the Arts Council has done, that theatres, opera companies and ballet should get their work on TV is precisely to miss the point of live theatre. Whole swathes of the population have been deterred from these art forms by seeing the miserably inert attempts to translate performances to TV which are inherently untranslatable. What is needed is the widespread opportunity to see the thing itself, and that means sustaining touring venues, giving the larger permanent theatre companies the resources and encouragement to tour, and adequately funding those companies for whom touring is their reason for existence.

It requires a great act of imagination to conjure up the vision of any of our political parties campaigning on the platform of huge increases in educational spending, let alone on the arts. Notwithstanding current proposals, the merest blink at the nation's balance sheet will reveal that there is only one pool of resources that could be skimmed: the defence budget. But in a country where you are publicly described as a traitor for questioning the wisdom of committing British forces to battle in the Gulf it takes a brave (or foolish) politician to speculate what might be done for the price of a Tornado or an F-111, let alone ask whether we need such a large number of military bands. Incidentally, owing to our infantile obsession with secrecy, this is a figure that is far from easy to uncover. Their cost, I gather from sources, is £66 million, or ten times the sum spent on our major orchestras. It is spent on eighty-one bands. I wonder who is monitoring *their* box office figures. But perhaps I am missing the point.

We have been encouraged to look to sponsorship as a secondary source of income and the arts world has now accepted its mixed economy. Yet for all its exhortation the government has done little to encourage the sponsor. To cite the American model *pour encourager les autres* is to ignore the much larger tax advantages, both personal and corporate, that it offers, and it's to be blind to the huge difference between a nation that believes in philanthropy out of gratitude or self-promotion, or even guilt, and a nation that, apart from a few outstanding contributions, has no tradition of private giving.

The state lottery is a recent recruit to the funding stakes. It appears to offer a new and unencumbered source of revenue. As somebody who spent many of his teenage years on a racecourse, and much of his university career in a betting shop, I can't pretend to a sense of moral outrage at the arts being sustained by gambling. I would, however, look warily at the example of the lottery as it has worked in several Australian states. There it provides money for sport, health (and *we're* complaining) and, running a poor third, the arts. For a while the lottery attracted a great deal of money, the state governments were able to divert their resources elsewhere, only to find that the revenue from the lottery flattened out, then diminished, leaving its clients worse off than they had been before. Some states also have a cigarette tax, the revenue of which goes directly to the arts. A sublime case of putting it in one's pipe and smoking it.

The unseemly spectacle of the scramble for television franchises, a sort of entrepreneurial version of the Eton Wall Game, has reminded us of Lord Thomson's famous dictum that 'television is a licence to print money'. Rather than turn our attentions to the tobacco companies we could do worse than oblige television companies, which should include the BBC, to pay something back to an industry which they draw on extensively for talent and inspiration.

There's a widespread belief that when we speak of money being provided for the arts we are asking for the money to hear the sound of our own voices echoing in an empty room. I know of no theatre in this country that treats with disdain the notion of finding an audience, or that is able to afford that luxury even if it were thought desirable. Most of our theatres depend on self-generated income for well over half of their revenue. At the National Theatre unless we earn nearly £13 million a year through our own efforts we are faced, like Mr Micawber, with the result: misery.

It is probably very English of me to feel that there is such a notion as excessive subsidy, that in the German theatre (at least prior to reunification) something *had* been lost in the relationship between the audience and the artists. In the end the German theatres were able to survive without the approval of their public; this is power without responsibility, the often cited cliché of the prostitute's role; a curious irony given the tone of high seriousness that pervades the German theatre.

My second question was this: Who will distribute the money to whom? Regardless of what I have said in criticism of the Arts Council, I believe that it is, like democracy, the least worst system on offer. Even if it often appears to its clients like Churchill's view of Russia, a riddle wrapped in a mystery inside an enigma, it is still preferable to a ministry whose decisions must, by definition, be subject to changes in political temperature. When its view of its own aims was clear, when it was given the money to carry out those aims, when there was a clear distance between the government and the Arts Council, it seemed to me to be one of those singular British institutions that worked as well in practice as in principle.

I don't believe that it is a sentimental desire for an Elysian past to wish for an Arts Council whose priorities are artistic rather than political, whose role is supervisory rather than regulatory, and whose manner towards its clients does not resemble that of social workers with habitual probationary recidivists. It would be an Arts Council that foreswore the temptation to involve itself in commercial ventures for which it has no brief and no expertise, and whose results have been as ill-fated as the notorious Ground Nut Scheme.

If this Arts Council were to be better funded it could do nothing more worthwhile for the theatre than to see that it implements in all respects the recommendations of its excellent strategy document, *The Cork Report*. It's subtitled *The Theatre* Is *for All*: national, regional, touring, commercial, amateur, educational, managerial and architectural. The blueprint is there; all that is needed is the will, the money, and the courage to make unpopular discriminatory judgements. This is only half the equation; we must prove on the other side that we have the imagination and the desire to create a theatre worthy of this lavish attention.

When the patient has been revived, when the theatres are occupied all the year round with plays rather than snooker tournaments; when there are theatres throughout the country which can perform the plays of Shakespeare with enough actors to avoid Claudius doubling the Ghost *and* the Gravedigger; when playwrights are offered productions rather than workshops; when there are, if not 37 million Molières, at least two dozen good playwrights under thirty who are not writing monologues for studio theatres but plays about whole worlds teeming with energy, we will still have to face the question of what we are saying with this multitude of voices. Whatever the writers write we can be certain of one thing: they will not write to an agenda set by administrators, politicians, sponsors, critics, or even theatre directors.

We live in the first atheistic age in history, which asserts that man is capable of knowing and doing anything. We no longer respect what we *don't* know, and the more we want to control the world the more despairing we feel when we find we are unable to control anything outside our homes, let alone within them. In this context art is hope; it is redemption.

To say such things in the eighties was to ask to be dragged to the stocks to be pelted with ridicule and accused of sententiousness, sanctimoniousness, but worst of all, of being boring. I am unapologetic. I am also hopeful that the nineties will see a world where to be serious about anything that is not profit-making is not a folly, and to talk of moral values in art is not a misdemeanour.

At heart, no art amounts to anything which doesn't give pleasure. We should always keep in mind the epitaph given to himself by Picasso, the artist who above all embodies the maelstrom of our century: 'I was only an entertainer who understood my times.'

EPILOGUE

In life, pretending to feel what we don't feel breeds bitterness – feigning interest when we're bored, being polite when we feel resentful, delighted when we're disappointed; but acting for a living breeds resilience and fortitude – in a word, stoicism. Working with actors daily, it's hard not to be infected by this philosophy. It's not necessarily an attractive doctrine, and to rely on endurance may not be a path to virtue, but at least it gets you through the night. 'An actor,' said Macready, 'must affect an immoderate bouyancy of spirits while perhaps his heart is breaking.'

Once I saw a performance by Ralph Richardson, and afterwards I told a friend of mine who was in the production how remarkable I thought he'd been. 'Yes, it's amazing,' she said. 'I saw him looking very melancholy before the show, and I said, "Are you all right, Ralph? You look very sad."' 'Oh, you know, I've had a bit of bad news,' he said. 'My brother's been killed. In a fire.' 'Oh Ralph,' she said, 'how awful.' 'Yes,' he said. 'Still, there's one consolation – it can't happen again.'

ACKNOWLEDGEMENTS

Grateful acknowledgement is given to the original publishers of the following pieces:

'Granville-Barker'
'Granville-Barker's Prefaces' – Nick Hern Books, 1992.

'Peter Brook'
'My Hero' – *Independent Magazine*, 1st April, 1989.

'Ken Campbell'
Independent, 28th February, 1992.

'Ian Charleson'
'Ian Charleson – A Tribute' – *Guardian*, 9th January, 1990.

'Ion Caramitru'
'Hamlet in Romania' – *Guardian*, 13th October, 1990.

'Tony Harrison'
'Tony Harrison – Such Men are Dangerous' –
Bloodaxe Books, 1991.

'Guys and Dolls' from *Guys and Dolls*, Methuen, 1992.

'Richard III (1990)',
with thanks to Dominique Goy-Blanquet.

'My Country Right or Wrong'
Sunday Telegraph, 1988.

'What's the National Theatre For?',
Independent, 1st October, 1988.

'What Are the Arts for?'
Speech at Arts Advocacy Day, 25th October, 1989,
Evening Standard, 26th October, 1989.

'Bonfires on the Moon',
Independent, 6th October, 1991.

There were several books which either filled gaps in my knowledge, or in my memory, when I was writing about my family: Edward Wilson's *Diary of the Discovery Expedition*, *Scott of the Antarctic* by Reginald Pound, *Signpost to Eyrecourt* by Ida Gantz, and *The Hero as Murderer* by Geoffrey Dutton. Above all, my gratitude is to my sister who lived through much of what I describe, and remembers some of it rather differently. My thanks also to my cousin, Kitty Clarke, who has the gift, or the curse, of perfect recall.

A NOTE ON THE AUTHOR

Richard Eyre has been Director of the Royal National Theatre since 1988. He has directed numerous premières including plays by David Hare, Alan Bennett, Christopher Hampton, Trevor Griffiths, Ken Campbell and Howard Brenton, and many classics, notably *Guys and Dolls*, *Richard III* and *Hamlet* (twice). He has produced and directed films for television, including *Tumbledown*, *The Insurance Man* and *The Ploughman's Lunch*.